It's another Quality Book from CGP

This book has been carefully written for 9-10 year olds.

It contains lots of questions covering all the Maths in the Year 5 Programme of Study — all perfectly matched to the National Curriculum for 2014 and beyond.

There are also practice tests at the start and end of the book to make sure you really know your stuff.

What CGP is all about

Our sole aim here at CGP is to produce the highest quality books — carefully written, immaculately presented and dangerously close to being funny.

Then we work our socks off to get them out to you — at the cheapest possible prices.

Contents

Section Four — Measurement

Section Five — Geometry

Section Six — Statistics

Published by CGP

Editors:
Katie Braid, Katherine Craig, Rob Harrison, Sarah Pattison, Camilla Simson.

Contributors:
Simon Greaves, Paul Warnes.

ISBN: 978 1 84762 213 6

With thanks to Karen Wells and Nicola Paddock for the proofreading.
Also thanks to Jan Greenway for the copyright research.

Thumb illustration used throughout the book © iStockphoto.com.

Printed by Elanders Ltd, Newcastle upon Tyne.
Clipart from Corel®

Based on the classic CGP style created by Richard Parsons.

About This Book

This Book is Full of Year 5 Maths Questions

You'll learn a lot of new maths in Year 5.
This book has questions on all the maths for Year 5. It matches our Year 5 Study Book. This can help you if you get stuck.

This book covers the Attainment Targets for Year 5 of the 2014 National Curriculum. The topics covered are roughly equivalent to the old Levels 3-5.

The questions in Sections 1-6 are all colour-coded to show how difficult they are.

1	2	3
Easy	Harder	Challenge

The answers to all of the questions are at the back of this book.

This book also has two Objectives Tests.
The one at the front of the book is to test that you remember the maths you learnt in Year 4. The test at the back of the book is to see how well you know the maths in this book.

There are Learning Objectives on All Pages

Learning objectives say what you should be able to do.
Use the tick circles to show how confident you feel.

I can win silver at the Olympics.

You can use the tick boxes for ongoing assessment to record which attainment targets have been met. Printable checklists of all the objectives can be found at www.cgpbooks.co.uk/primarymaths.

Tick here if you think you need a bit more practice.

If you're really struggling, tick here.

Tick this circle if you can do all the maths on the page.

"I can subtract 1s, 10s and 100s from a 3-digit number."

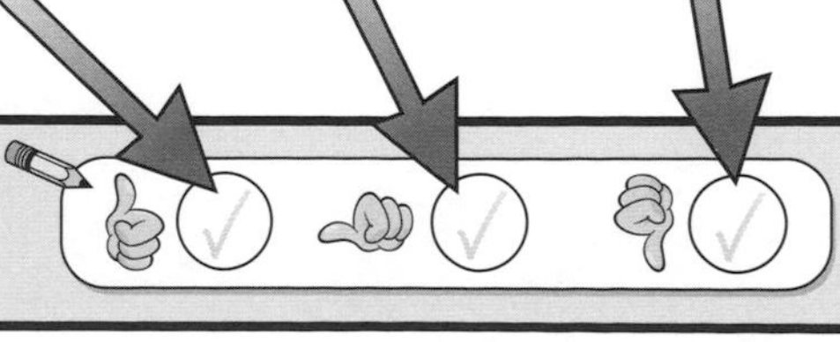

Year Four Objectives Test

1 Round 1.6 to the nearest whole number.

1 mark

2 The grid below is made up of squares with sides of 1 cm.
Draw a rectangle with an area of 12 square centimetres.

1 mark

3 Alison checks her watch when she finishes work.

What time does it show?
Circle the correct answer.

15:35 5:07 19:25 17:25

1 mark

Alison cycles home from work. It takes her an hour and a quarter.

How many minutes is this?

minutes

1 mark

4 Pencils cost 25p each and pens cost 48p each.

Lucy has a 50p coin and two 20p coins.
She buys a pencil and a pen.
How much money does she have left? Show your working.

p

2 marks

5 Circle the decimal that is equivalent to $\frac{1}{10}$.

0.0 **0.2** **1.0** **0.1** **0.3**

1 mark

6 Write the Roman numerals below as numbers.

XCII =

XIX =

2 marks

7 Karen lives 0.45 km from the shops.

How far is this in metres?

m

1 mark

8 The temperature in Florida is 25 °C. The temperature in Moscow is –12 °C.
What is the difference between the two temperatures?

°C

1 mark

9 A restaurant sells 3 types of pizza.
The chart shows how many of each were sold on Saturday.

cheese	⊕ ⊕ ⊕ ◔ (3¾ symbols)
ham	⊕ ⊕ ◔ (2¼ symbols)
salami	⊕ ⊕ ⊕ ⊕ ◑ (4½ symbols)

⊕ = 4 pizzas

The restaurant sold 12 salami pizzas on Friday.

How many more salami pizzas did it sell on Saturday than on Friday?

[ ] salami pizzas

1 mark

The restaurant sold twice as many ham pizzas on Friday as on Saturday.

How many ham pizzas did it sell on Friday?

[ ] ham pizzas

1 mark

10 Write these decimals in order, from smallest to largest.

23.04 0.16 1.44 0.11 0.07 5.15

[ ] [ ] [ ] [ ] [ ] [ ]

smallest ⟶ largest

1 mark

11 Fill in the empty boxes to complete the equivalent fractions.

$\frac{\square}{8} = \frac{3}{4}$ $\frac{5}{15} = \frac{1}{\square}$ $\frac{1}{2} = \frac{\square}{18}$

2 marks

12 Fill in the empty boxes in the grid below.

×	3	☐	4
7	21	42	28
☐	24	48	32

1 mark

13 Reece measures how far he can kick a football.

On the first kick the ball goes 25.4 m.
On the second kick the ball goes 6.7 m further.

How far did he kick the ball the second time?

m

1 mark

14 Calculate $\frac{5}{6}$ of 72.

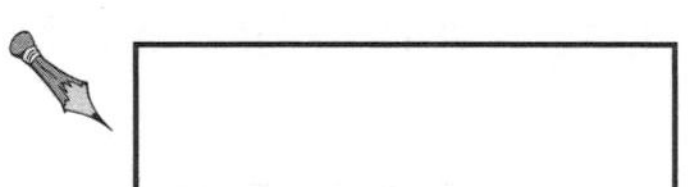

1 mark

15 This shape is made up of identical rectangles.

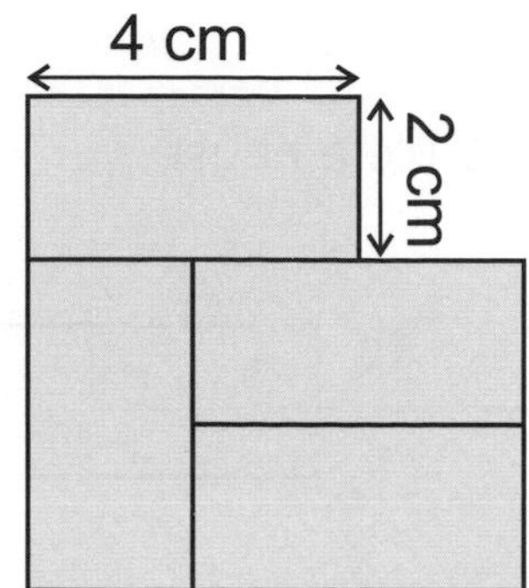

Find its perimeter.

cm

1 mark

Total

Counting Backwards Through Zero

1 Work out these calculations. Use the number line to help you.

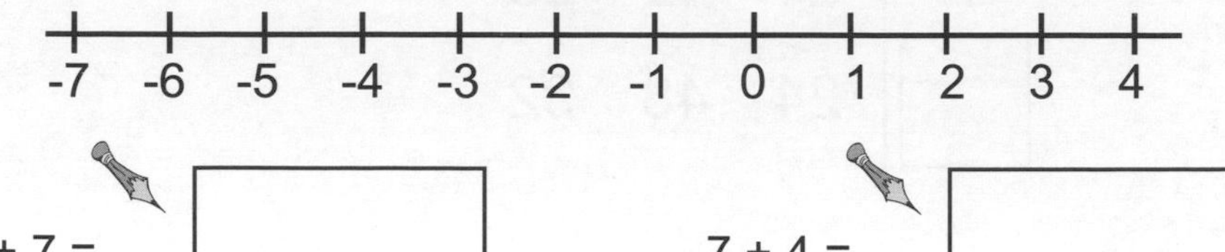

–5 + 7 = ☐ –7 + 4 = ☐

2 marks

2 Look at this thermometer.

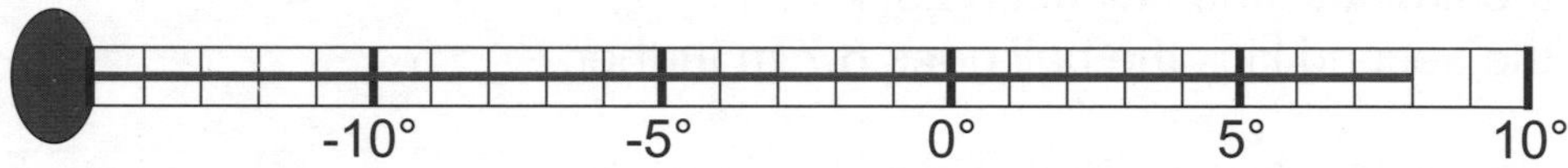

Fill in the missing numbers.

The temperature now is ☐ °C.

If the temperature fell by 14 °C it would be ☐ °C.

2 marks

3 What temperature is 24 degrees lower than 10 °C?

Use the number line to help you.

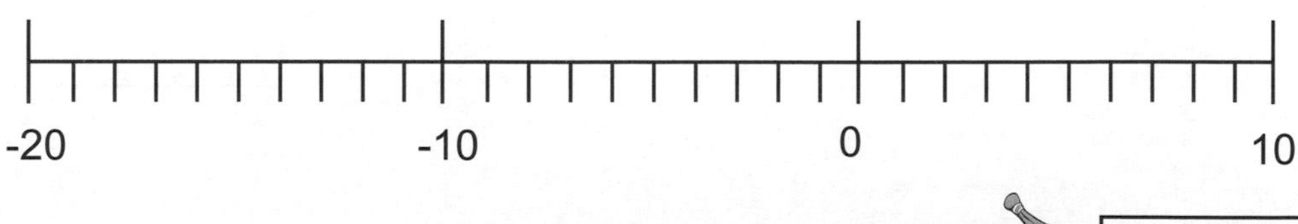

☐ °C

1 mark

4 Two thermometers show the temperature inside and outside a house.

Thermometer A shows a temperature of 25 °C.
Thermometer B shows a temperature of -13 °C.
What is the difference between the two temperatures?

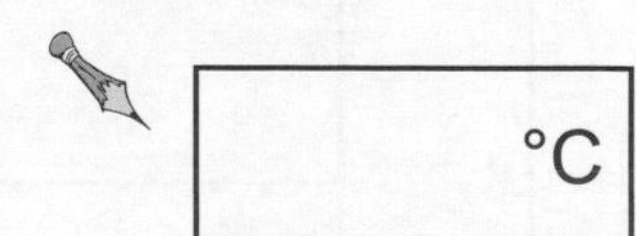

1 mark

"I can count backwards and forwards through zero, and solve problems with negative numbers in."

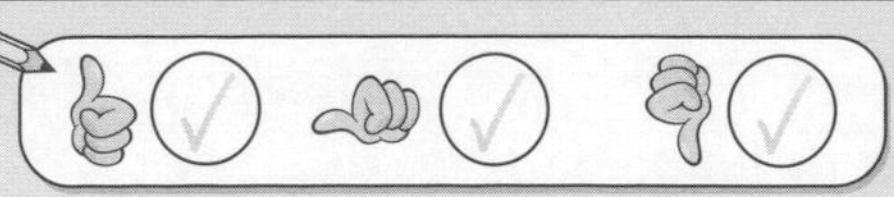

Place Value in Big Numbers

1 What is the value of each of these digits in 654 321?

Write your answers in the boxes.

4 [ ] 1 mark

6 [ ] 1 mark

2 [ ] 1 mark

2 Yvonne won £126 547 in a raffle.

In words write out how much money she won.

[ ] pounds 1 mark

3 Write out in numbers the following amounts.

Five million, two hundred and forty eight thousand and sixty three.

[ ] 1 mark

Seven hundred and eleven thousand, nine hundred and seven.

[ ] 1 mark

4 Use partitioning to complete this sum:

89490 = [ ] + [ ] + 400 + [ ] 1 mark

"I can read, write and partition numbers up to a million."

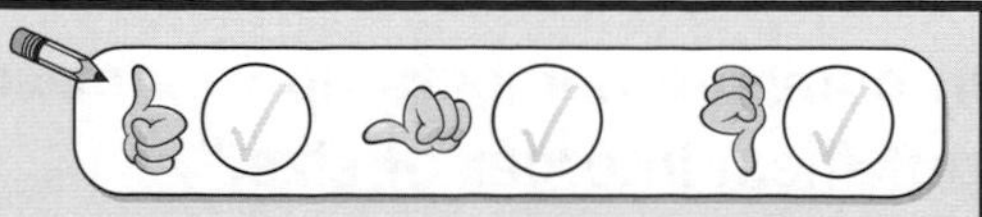

Ordering and Comparing Big Numbers

1 Look at these numbers. Write < or > in each box.

217 563 ☐ 271 236　　575 896 ☐ 758 962

924 567 ☐ 924 537　　223 237 ☐ 224 237

2 marks

2 The table below shows the number of golf balls a company sold over five years.

	Number of Golf Balls Sold
Year 1	921 455
Year 2	487 217
Year 3	397 181
Year 4	489 006
Year 5	921 269

Which year were the most golf balls sold?

1 mark

Which year were the fewest golf balls sold?

1 mark

Write < or > in the box to complete this sentence:

The number of golf balls sold in Year 2 was ☐ the number sold in Year 4.

1 mark

3 Put these numbers in ascending order.

217 569　　216 452　　318 569　　21 989

Write the numbers in the boxes.

☐ ☐ ☐ ☐

smallest ⟶ largest

1 mark

"I can compare numbers up to a million and put them in order of size."

Counting in Powers of 10

1 Circle the numbers that are powers of 10.

400 1000 1 000 050 20 000 10

25 1 000 000 100 700 000

1 mark

2 Fill in the gaps in the sequence by counting up in steps of 1000.

15 572 [ ] [ ] [ ] 19 572

1 mark

3 Fill in the gaps in the sequence by counting down in steps of 100 000.

3 242 001 [ ] [ ] [ ] 2 842 001

1 mark

4 From 4 027 817, count down in steps of 1 000 000. Stop at 27 817.

1 mark

5 Count up from 888 453 in steps of 10 000. Stop after four steps.

1 mark

"I can count forwards or backwards in thousands, tens of thousands, hundreds of thousands, or millions."

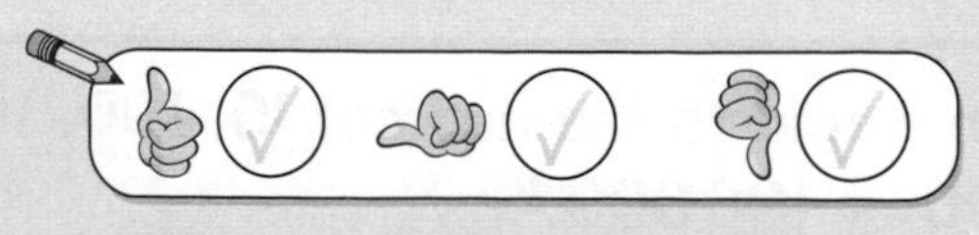

Rounding

1 2537 people went to the funfair on Saturday night.

Round this number to:

the nearest thousand. 1 mark

the nearest hundred. 1 mark

the nearest ten. 1 mark

2 The table below shows the top three scores on a computer game.

Round each score to the nearest ten thousand.

	'Escape from Zombie Jungle' Top Scores
1st	13 778 201
2nd	13 515 539
3rd	12 204 676

1 mark

1 mark

1 mark

3 755 046 tadpoles live in a swamp.

Round this number to:

the nearest thousand. 1 mark

the nearest ten thousand. 1 mark

the nearest hundred thousand. 1 mark

"I can round to the nearest 10, 100, 1000, 10 000 or 100 000."

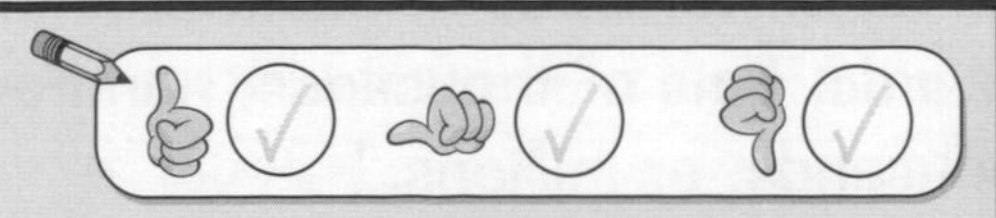

Roman Numerals

1 Fill in the gaps in the table below.

Roman Numeral	Number
M	
D	
X	
L	

2 marks

2 Draw lines to match each Roman numeral with the number it represents. The first one has been done for you.

LXXXIV CMX II LXIII DCCLXXVII

63 777 84 2 910

2 marks

3 Write out the following Roman numerals in numbers:

CCLXXXIII

XCIX

CMLXXXV

CXXV

2 marks

4 These years are given as Roman numerals. Write them out as numbers.

MCMLXXXVIII

MMLV

MCMLVIII

MCMXII

2 marks

"I can read Roman numerals up to M, and recognise years written in Roman numerals."

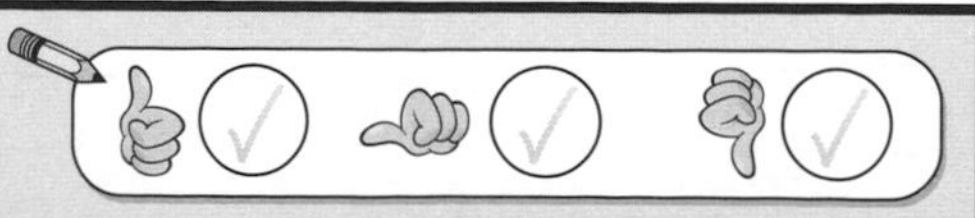

Written Adding and Subtracting

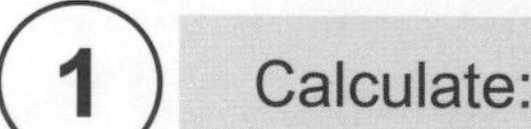

1 Calculate:

21 508 + 13 942

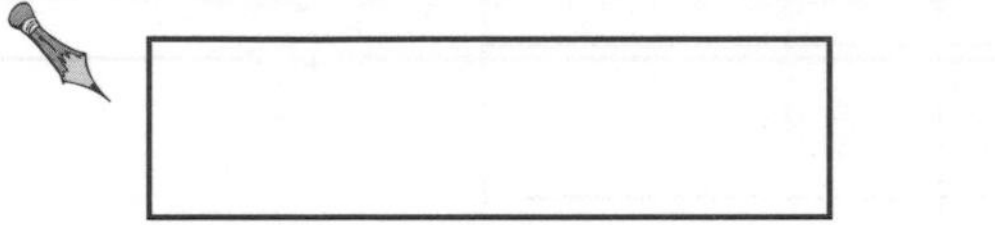

24 971 – 5433

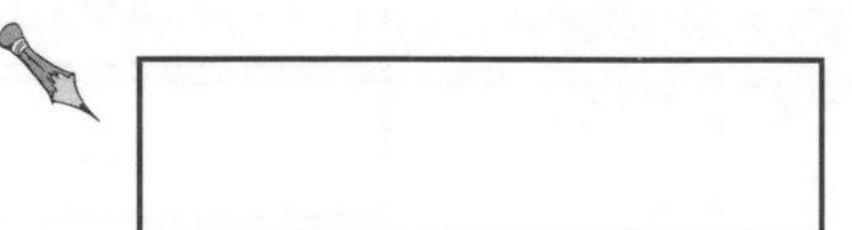

2 marks

2 At a recent football match, 17 930 spectators were supporting Barrow FC and 11 746 were supporting Barrow United.

How many spectators were there altogether?

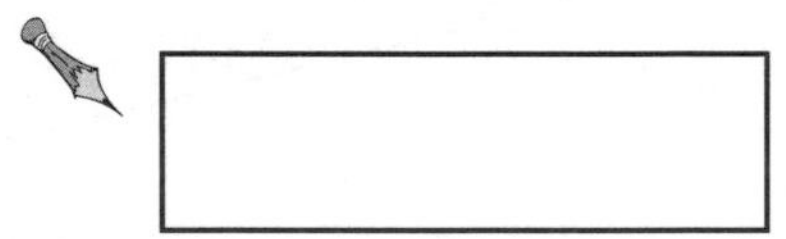

1 mark

3 Celia inherits £22 350. She gives £5365 to charity.

How much money does she have left?

1 mark

4 Fill in the missing numbers.

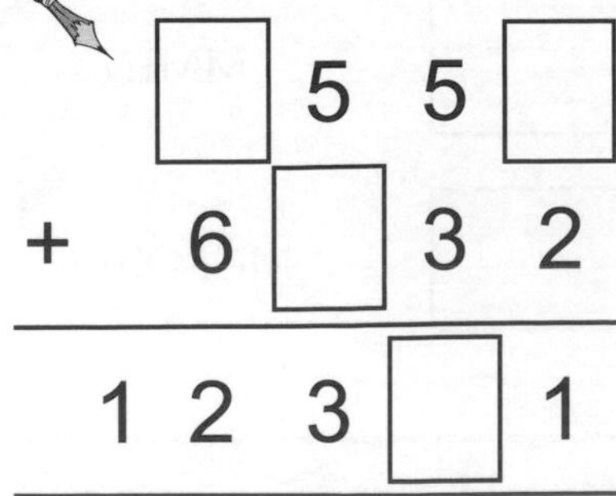

2 marks

Written Adding and Subtracting

5 Here are two items for sale at Broughton Electricals.

£9.95 £67.59

Dani buys both items. What is the total cost?
Show your working.

£

1 mark

6 Ben, Rajesh, Liam and Tom run the 100 m and 200 m races.

Their times for each race are shown in the table.

	100 m	200 m
Ben	12.56 s	26.61 s
Rajesh	13.11 s	26.81 s
Liam	14.66 s	29.05 s
Tom	13.40 s	27.68 s

Find the difference between the fastest and slowest times for the 100 m.

seconds

1 mark

How much longer did it take Liam to run 200 m than 100 m?

seconds

1 mark

"I can use standard written methods to add and subtract numbers."

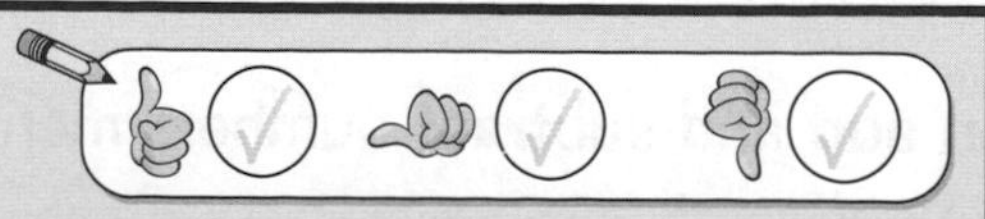

Mental Adding and Subtracting

This page is on **mental** maths, so you need to do these calculations in your head.

1 Work out:

2998 – 1050 = ☐ 1360 + 926 = ☐

2 marks

1564 + 362 = ☐ 5080 – 2090 = ☐

2 marks

2 What is 4.7 – 2.6?

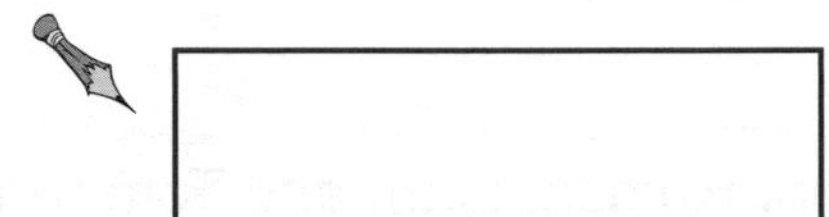

1 mark

3 Lucas is thinking of a number.
He adds 3500 to the number and then subtracts 15.

His answer is 76 842. What was the original number?

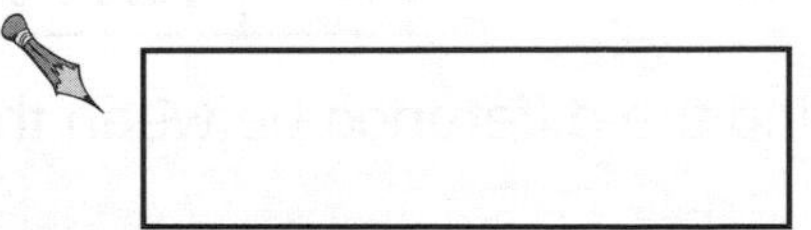

1 mark

4 Kinga walks 4.35 km on one day and 3.5 km on the next day.

How far does she walk altogether?

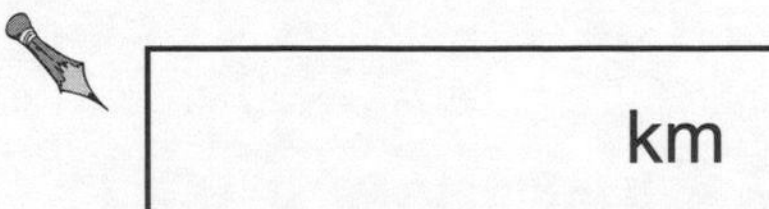

1 mark

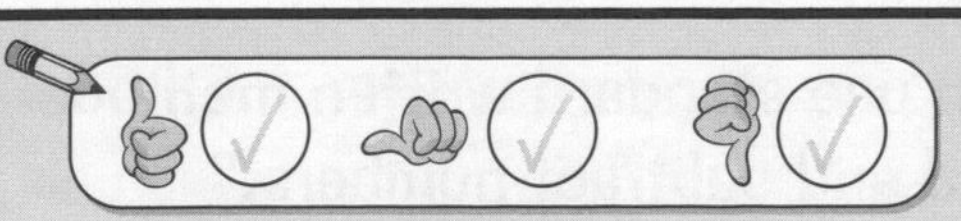

"I can add and subtract numbers mentally."

Rounding and Checking

1 At the beginning of the month, Petra's sunflower was 119.6 cm tall. At the end of the month it was 224.5 cm tall.

Estimate how much the sunflower had grown over the month.

cm

1 mark

2 Circle the best estimate to the answer to 55.71 ÷ 6.93.

7 8 9 10 11

1 mark

3 Hassan multiplies 6.21 by 4.88. He gets the answer 30.256.

Estimate the answer to 6.21 × 4.88. Is Hassan's answer reasonable?

Circle YES or NO

1 mark

Write a division that Hassan could do to check his answer.

1 mark

4 Adam buys 7 bags of apples. The total cost is £16.17.

Adam says, "£16.17 ÷ 7 = £2.31, so each bag of apples cost £2.31."
What calculation could he use to check his answer?

1 mark

"I can round numbers to check my answers, and I can check that my answers are sensible."

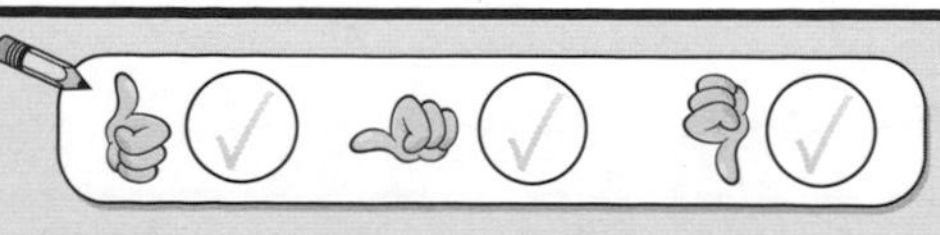

Square and Cube Numbers

1 Fill in the missing numbers.

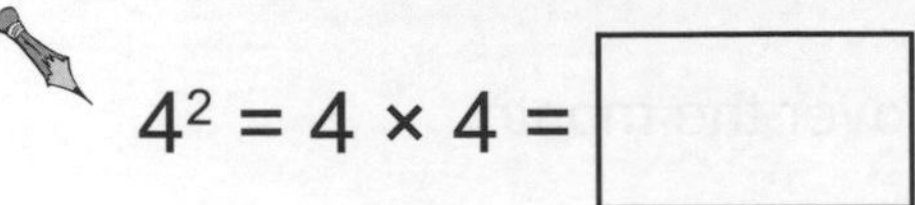

$4^2 = 4 \times 4 =$ ☐

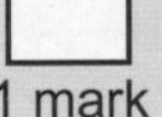

1 mark

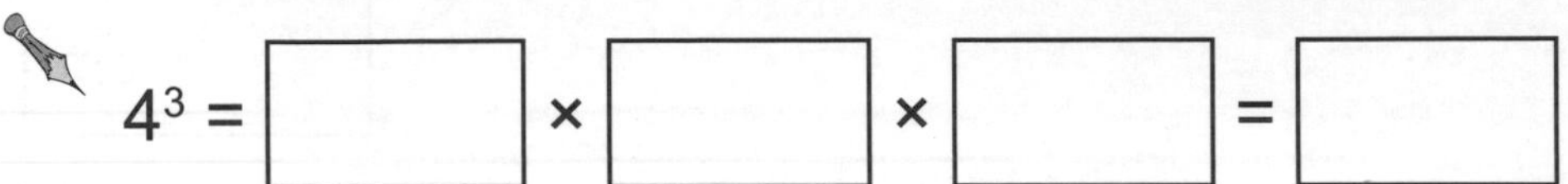

$4^3 =$ ☐ × ☐ × ☐ = ☐

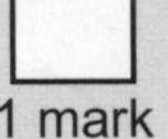

1 mark

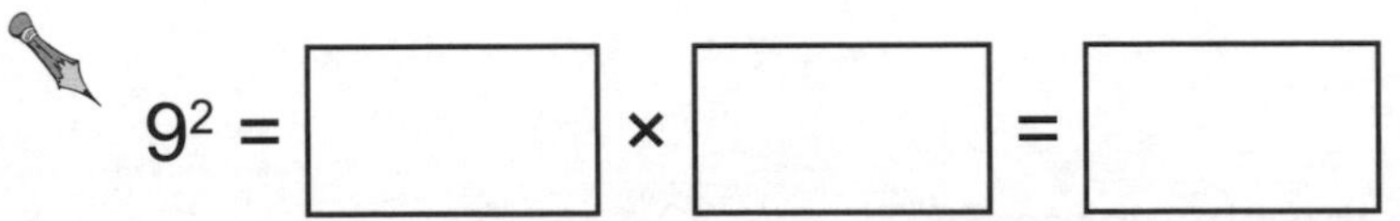

$9^2 =$ ☐ × ☐ = ☐

1 mark

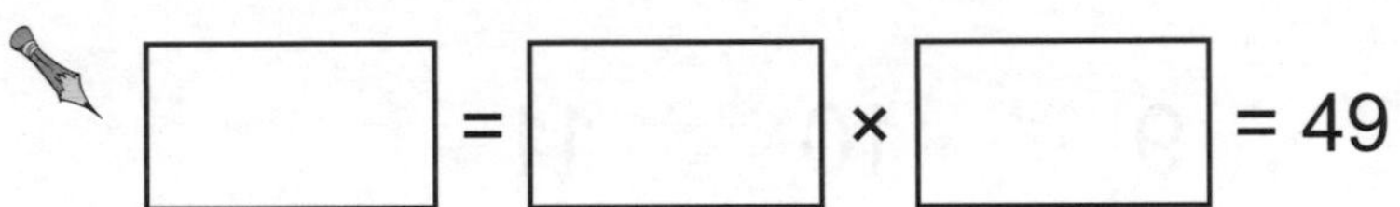

☐ = ☐ × ☐ = 49

1 mark

2 Fill in the missing number in this sequence.

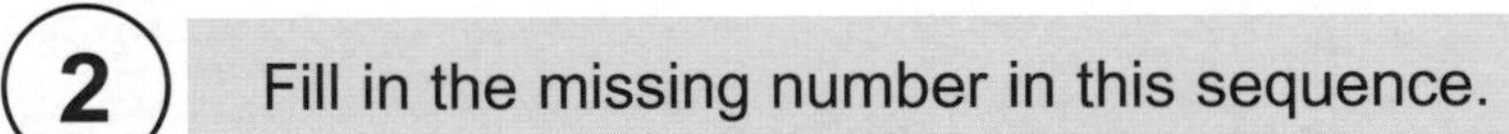

nine sixteen twenty five ☐ forty nine

1 mark

3 What is 5 cubed? Circle the correct answer.

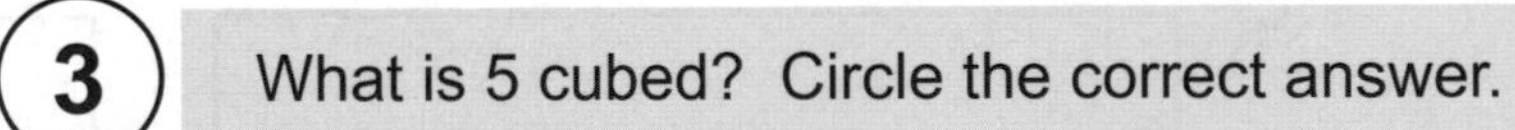

215 25 100 125 55 250

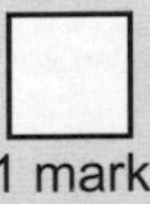

1 mark

4 Work out:

$3^2 + 5^2$

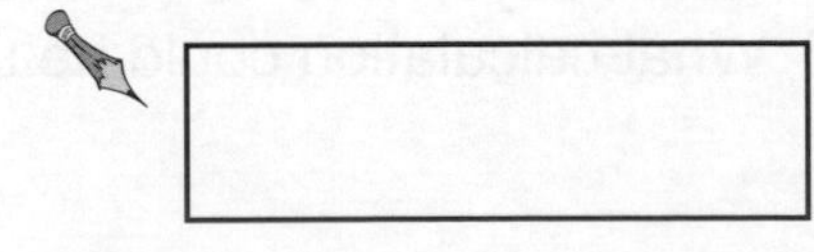

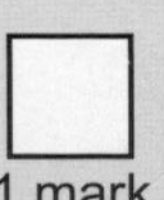

1 mark

$3^3 - 2^2$

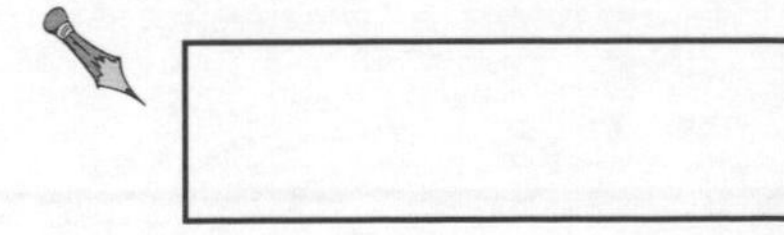

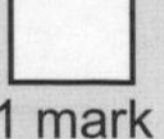

1 mark

Square and Cube Numbers

5 Calculate $6^2 + 8^2$.

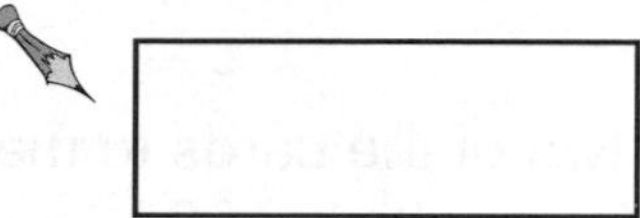

1 mark

Is your answer another square number? Circle: YES or NO

1 mark

Write a square number in each box to make this calculation correct:

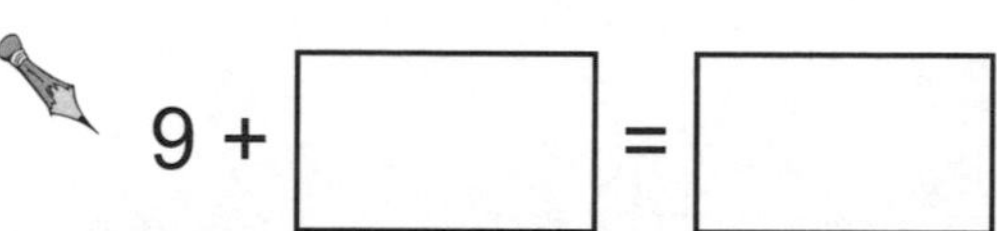

1 mark

6 Put a square number in each box to make these calculations correct.

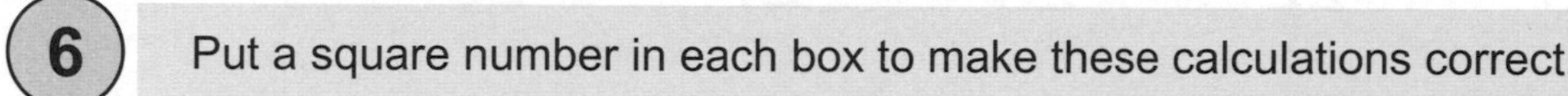

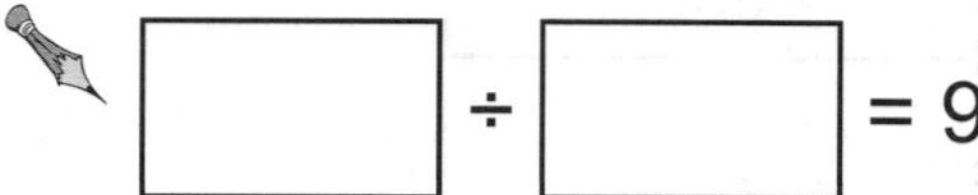

3 marks

7 Horace says, "56 is a cube number."

Use two cube numbers that you know to explain why Horace is not correct.

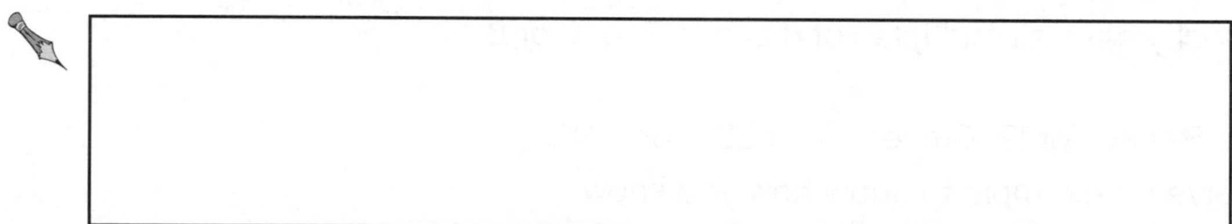

2 marks

8 There are two ways of adding two square numbers to make 65.

Write a different square number in each box.

☐ + ☐ = 65

and ☐ + ☐ = 65

2 marks

"I can recognise and use square and cube numbers."

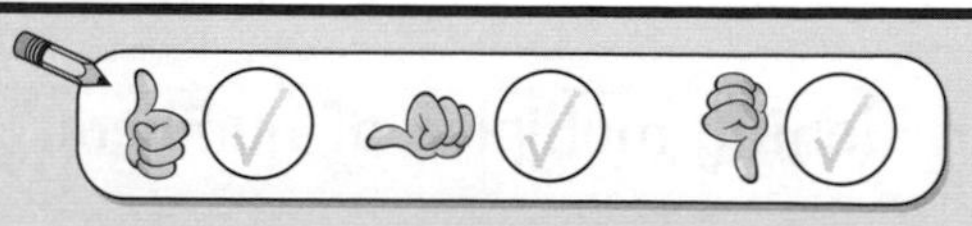

Multiples

1 Look at these four digit cards. 4 7 1 2

Use two of the cards to make a two-digit number that is a multiple of 9.

1 mark

2 Circle all the multiples of 4 on this list.

16 22 24 27 29

1 mark

3 Put a number less than 30 in each section of the table.

	multiple of 7	not a multiple of 7
even		
not even		

2 marks

4 Becky says all multiples of 8 end in 2, 4, 6 or 8.

Is Becky right? Circle: YES or NO.
Give an example to show how you know.

2 marks

5 Find a common multiple of 6 and 8.

1 mark

"I can identify multiples of numbers."

Factors and Primes

1 Circle the numbers that are factors of 28.

4 8 6 7 9 2

1 mark

2 List all the factor pairs of these numbers.

The first one has been done for you.

32

= 1 × 32
2 × 16
4 × 8

18

24

2 marks

3 Here are some numbers.

5 4 3 9 7

Which of these numbers is:

a factor of 32?

1 mark

a common factor of 12 and 21?

1 mark

4 Circle the prime numbers in this list.

9 13 15 21 26 29 54 61 73

2 marks

Factors and Primes

5 Write down the common factors of 16 and 20.

1 mark

6 Write a prime number in each box to make these calculations correct.

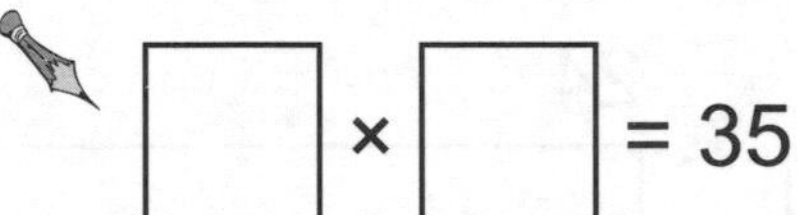

2 marks

7 Which two prime numbers are factors of all these numbers?

12 18 24 36 48

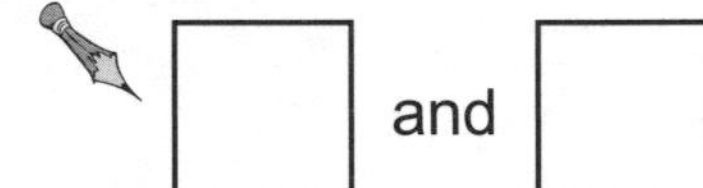

1 mark

8 These diagrams are called factor trees.

Each number is split into two factors. These factors are written in the boxes underneath the number. This is done until only prime numbers are left.

One of the factor trees below has been done for you.
Complete the second factor tree.

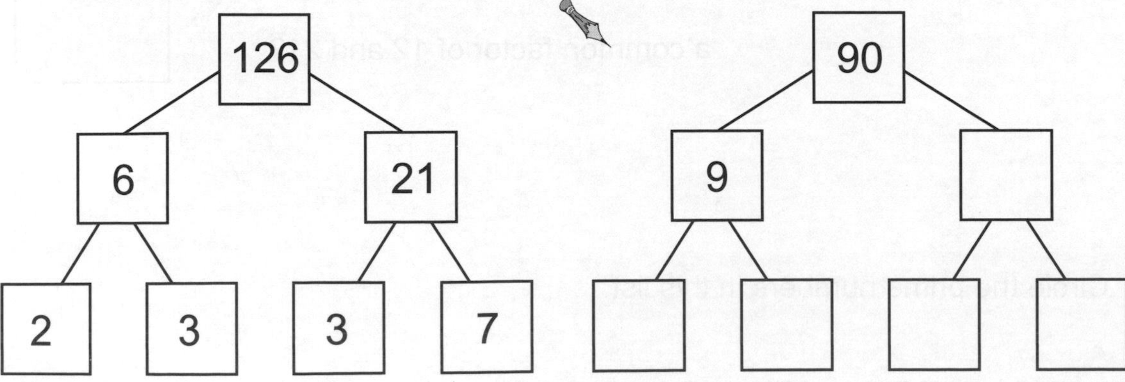

2 marks

"I can spot prime numbers up to 100. I can find factor pairs, common factors and prime factors."

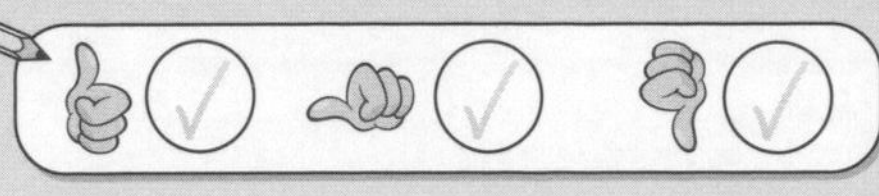

Multiplying and Dividing by 10, 100 and 1000

1 What is zero point eight seven multiplied by one thousand?

1 mark

2 Jamal thinks of a number. He divides it by 100. His answer is 3.64.

What number did Jamal think of?

1 mark

3 Mark has sold 1000 tickets for a raffle. They were sold in books of ten.

In total Mark collected £375 for all 1000 tickets.
How much did one book cost?

£

1 mark

4 Helen has some pens and some square tiles.

Each pen is 130 mm long. The sides of each tile are 13 mm long.

130 mm 13 mm

Helen lays 10 pens end to end to make a straight line.
She makes a line of tiles which is the same length as the line of pens.
How many tiles does she use?

tiles

1 mark

Multiplying and Dividing by 10, 100 and 1000

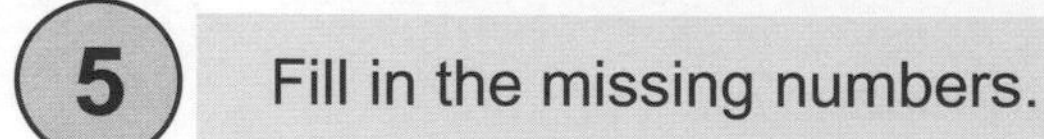

5 Fill in the missing numbers.

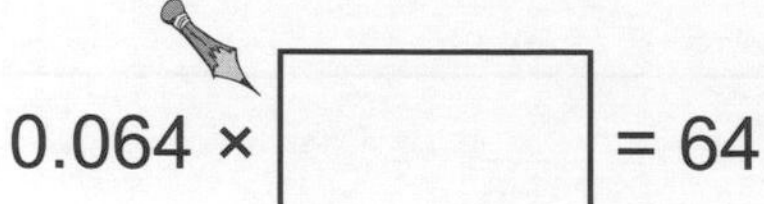

0.064 × ☐ = 64 10 × ☐ × 1.75 = 1750

☐ × 100 = 72.6 16 549 ÷ ☐ = 165.49

2 marks

6 Scott divides some 4-digit numbers by 1000.

His answer is a decimal every time.
Scott says, "If you divide a 4-digit number by 1000, the answer will never be a whole number."

Is Scott correct? Circle YES or NO
Give an example to show how you know.

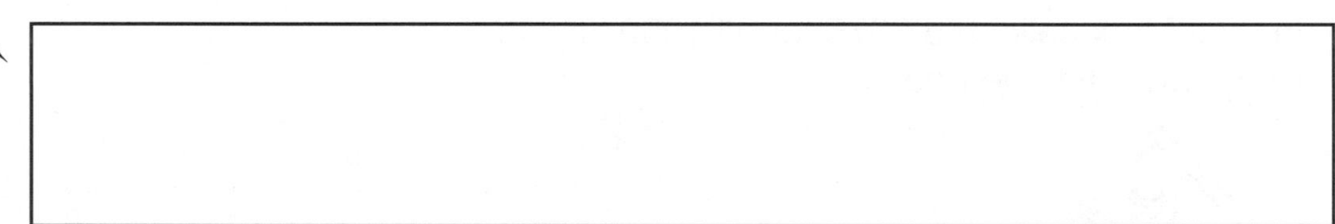

1 mark

7 Sara has some identical square tiles.

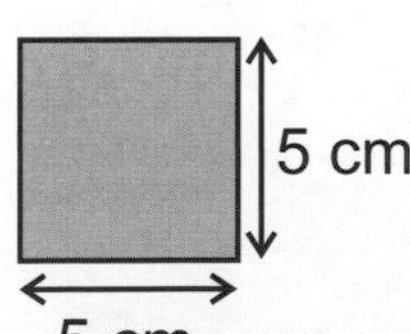

The area of this tile is 5 cm × 5 cm = 25 cm^2.
Sara makes a rectangle by laying out five rows of tiles.
There are twenty tiles in each row.

What is the area of Sara's rectangle? Show your working.

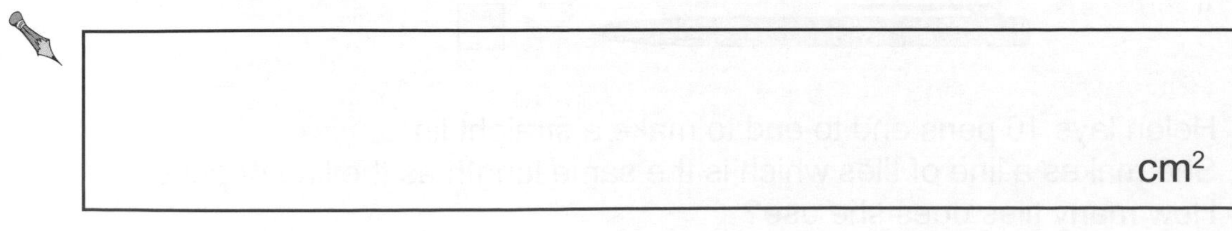

2 marks

"I can multiply and divide a whole number or decimal by 10, 100 or 1000."

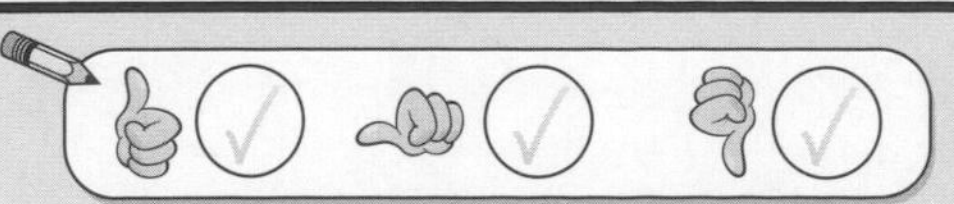

Mental Multiplying and Dividing

This page is on **mental** maths, so you need to work the answers out in your head.

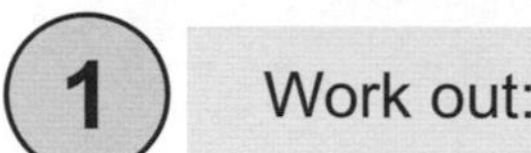

1 Work out:

84 ÷ 6

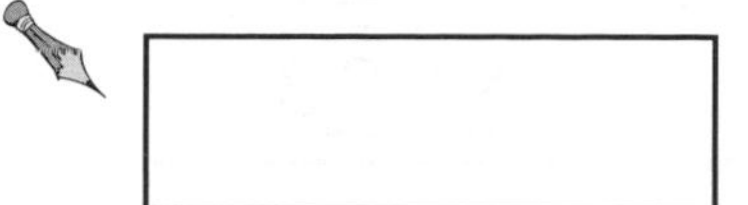

1 mark

84 ÷ 14

1 mark

2 Write the answers to these calculations:

8 × 25 = ☐ 17 × 4 = ☐

2 marks

3 4 bottles of lemonade cost £2.40.

How much does one bottle cost?

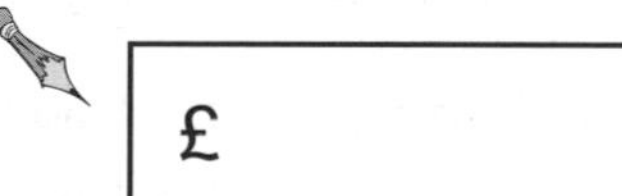

1 mark

4 Ash buys a box of pencils costing 68p.

How much would 6 boxes cost?

1 mark

5 A musician is paid £38.50 per hour.

How much will he earn for a 4 hour concert?

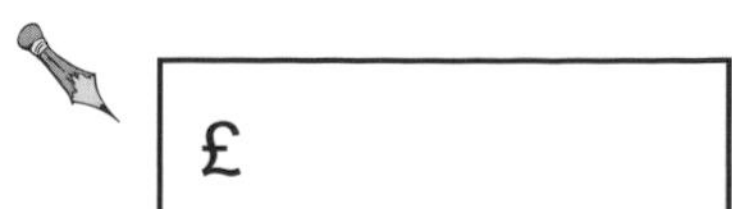

1 mark

"I can solve problems by multiplying and dividing in my head."

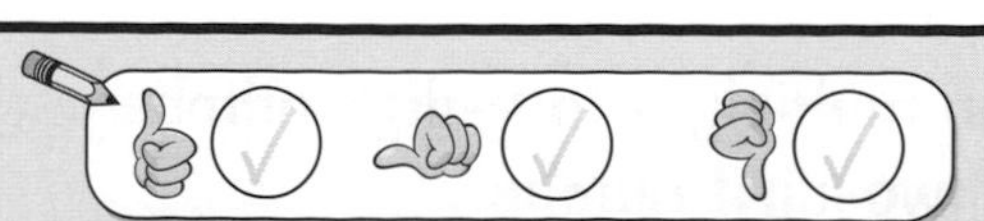

Written Multiplication

1 Calculate:

$$\begin{array}{r} 158 \\ \times\ 23 \\ \hline \end{array}$$

$$\begin{array}{r} 587 \\ \times\ 32 \\ \hline \end{array}$$

1349×12

3 marks

2 A television costs £369.

What is the total cost of 24 televisions?

£

1 mark

3 136 children are having a party.

Each child pays 75p towards food and drink.
How much money is this in total? Show your working.

£

1 mark

4 A box contains 2137 packets of screws. Each pack has 24 screws in it.

How many screws does the box contain altogether?
Show your working clearly.

screws

1 mark

"I can multiply a four-digit number by a two-digit number."

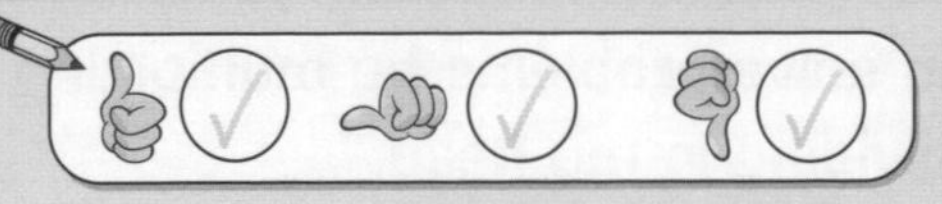

Written Division

1 What is 651 ÷ 7?

1 mark

2 Calculate these divisions.

858 ÷ 6

1 mark

2315 ÷ 5

1 mark

3 What is 3238 ÷ 4?

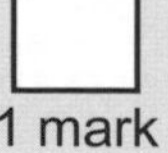

1 mark

4 What is two thousand, two hundred and fifty six divided by seven?

Write the remainder as a fraction.

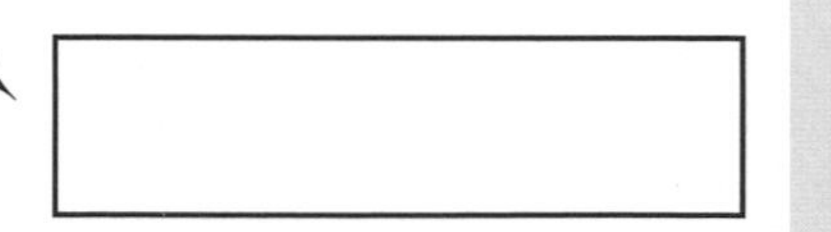

1 mark

5 Tennis balls are packed into boxes of 8.

A sports club needs 1150 tennis balls. How many boxes should they buy?

1 mark

"I can divide a four-digit number by a one-digit number and deal with remainders."

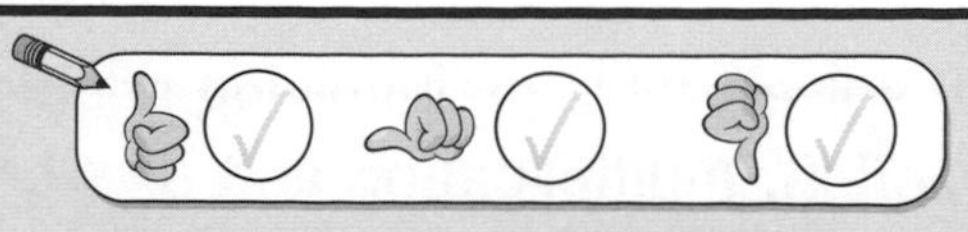

Solving Calculation Problems

1 Gavin has 180 sweets. He keeps 40 for himself and shares the rest out between 6 friends so that each person gets an equal number.

How many sweets does each friend get?

sweets

1 mark

How many sweets are left over?

sweets

1 mark

2 Omar works 30 hours a week and is paid £8 per hour.

How much does he earn per week?

£

1 mark

Jess is paid three quarters of the amount that Omar is paid.
How much does she earn in 5 hours?

£

1 mark

3 Gwen buys a shirt for £12.95 and a hat for £3.99.

How much change does she get from a £20 note?

£

1 mark

4 Amy and Ben are baking for a cake sale.
Amy bakes for three hours and makes 60 cakes an hour.
Ben takes two hours to bake the same amount of cakes.

How many cakes does Ben make per hour?

cakes

1 mark

"I can solve problems involving addition, subtraction, multiplication and division."

Thousandths

1 Write these numbers as a fraction:

Five thousandths

Twenty three thousandths

2 marks

2 Choose from the numbers below to fill in the blanks.

0.03 0.4 0.3 0.004 0.13 0.04

three hundredths =

$\frac{3}{10}$ =

$\frac{4}{1000}$ =

13 hundredths =

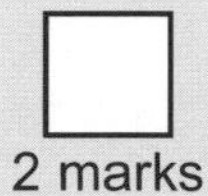

2 marks

3 Here is a list of numbers.

2.18 2.02 2.073 2.116

Write these numbers in the correct boxes on the number line below.

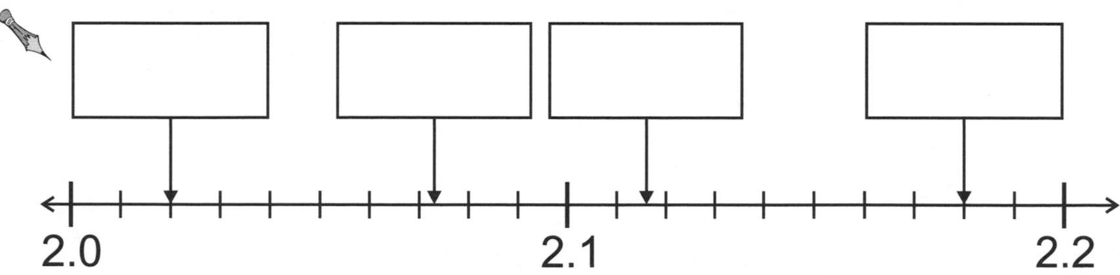

1 mark

4 Circle the decimal that is equivalent to $\frac{12}{1000}$.

0.12 0.2 0.21 1.2 0.012 0.002

1 mark

"I can write thousandths as fractions or decimals."

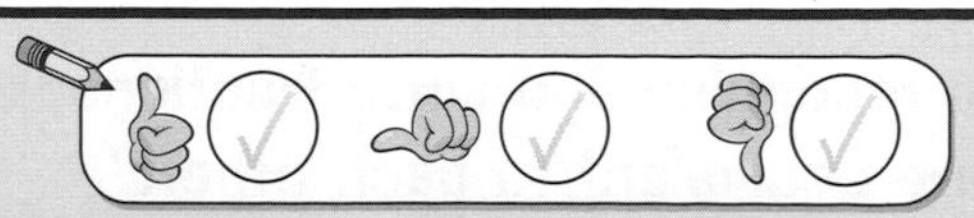

Equivalent Fractions

1 Shade $\frac{2}{5}$ of each of these shapes.

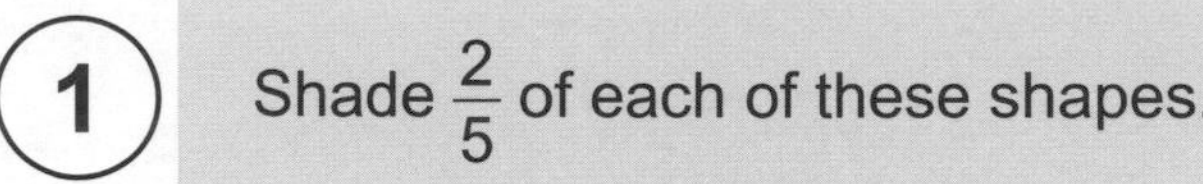

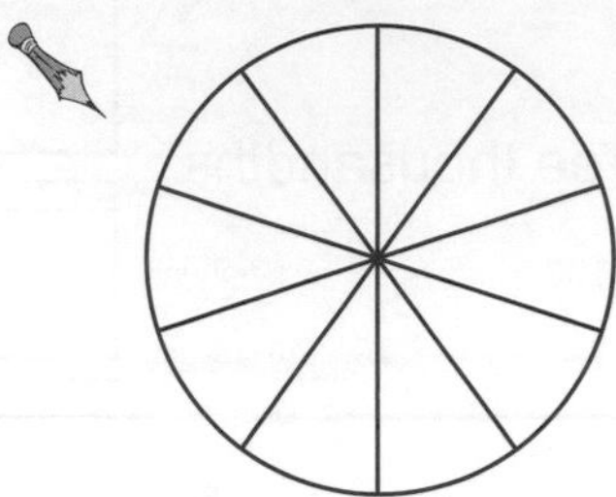

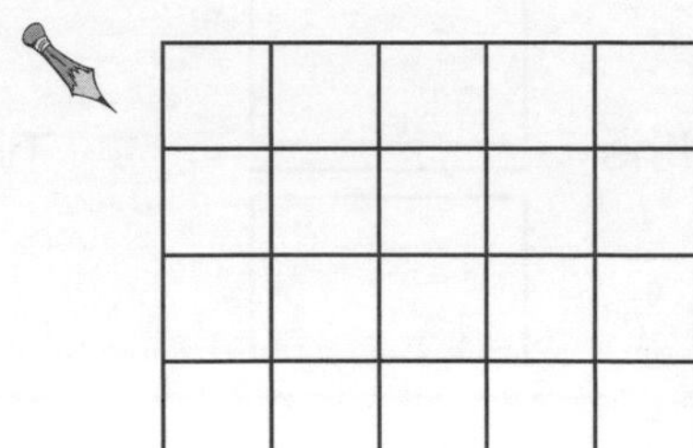

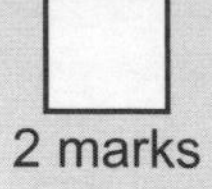

2 Complete these equivalent fractions.

$$\frac{1}{4} = \frac{\square}{8} = \frac{\square}{12} = \frac{4}{\square} = \frac{5}{\square} = \frac{6}{\square}$$

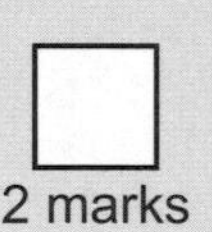

3 Write six tenths...

...in hundredths. $\frac{\square}{\square}$

...in fifths. $\frac{\square}{\square}$

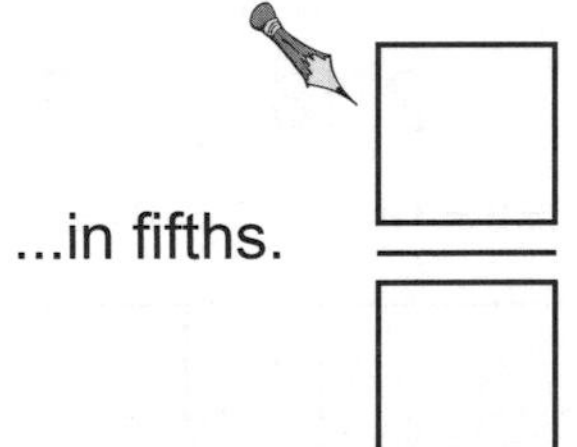

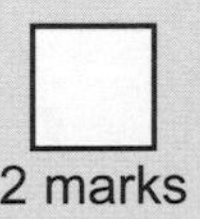

4 Fill in the boxes to make the fractions equivalent.

$$\frac{\square}{8} = \frac{14}{16} = \frac{35}{\square}$$

1 mark

"I can recognise and write fractions that are equivalent to each other."

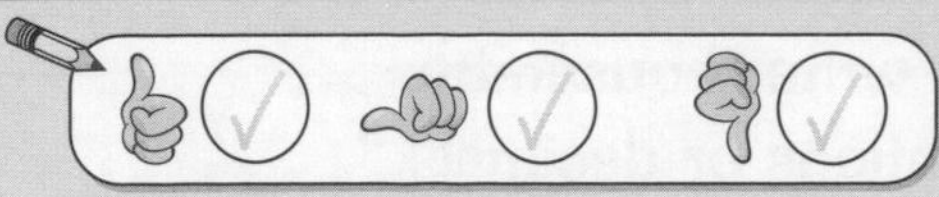

Ordering Fractions

1 Circle the larger fraction in each pair.

$\frac{7}{14}$ or $\frac{2}{14}$ $\qquad$ $\frac{3}{20}$ or $\frac{8}{20}$

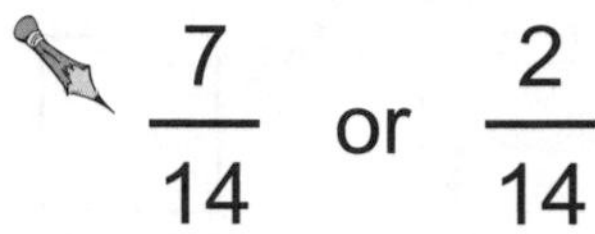

$\frac{1}{6}$ or $\frac{4}{12}$ $\qquad$ $\frac{2}{10}$ or $\frac{15}{100}$

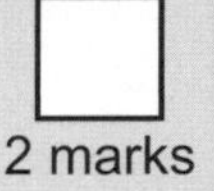

2 marks

2 Put the fractions $\frac{3}{4}$, $\frac{2}{8}$ and $\frac{8}{16}$ in order, from smallest to largest.

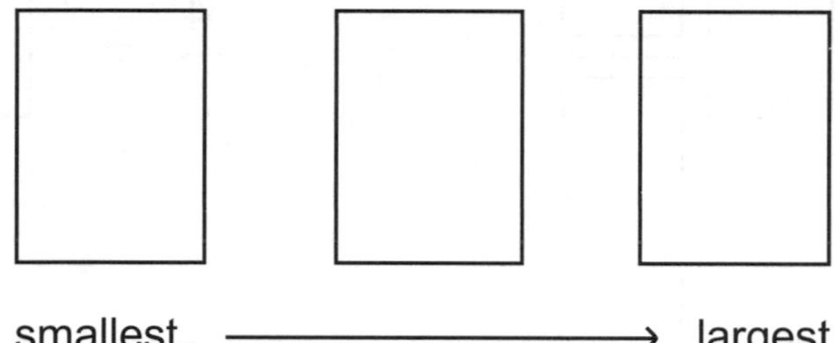

smallest ⟶ largest

1 mark

3 Write these fractions in order of size.

$\frac{4}{10}$ $\qquad$ $\frac{10}{15}$ $\qquad$ $\frac{3}{5}$ $\qquad$ $\frac{14}{30}$ $\qquad$ $\frac{16}{20}$

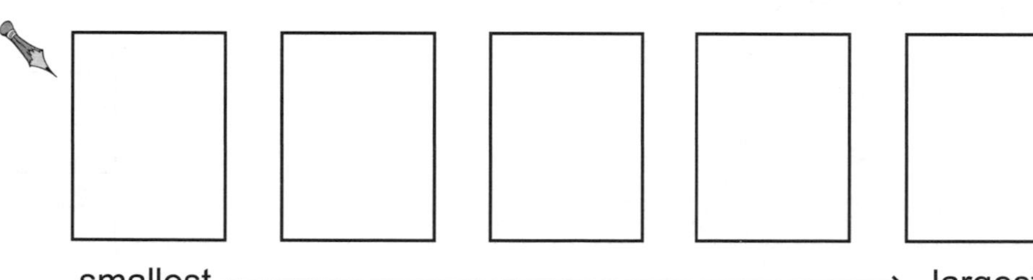

smallest ⟶ largest

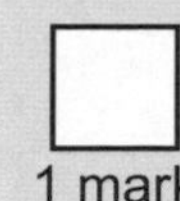

1 mark

4 Celia walks $\frac{3}{7}$ of a mile to work and Graham walks $\frac{4}{9}$ of a mile.

Who walks the furthest?

1 mark

"I can compare fractions and order them by their size."

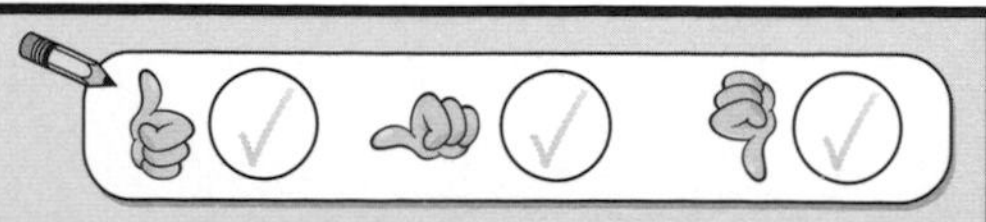

Adding and Subtracting Fractions

1 

Calculate:

$\frac{2}{10} + \frac{7}{10} = \frac{\square}{\square}$ $\frac{9}{15} - \frac{4}{15} = \frac{\square}{\square}$

2 marks

2 Write these improper fractions as mixed numbers.

$\frac{13}{10} = \square\frac{\square}{\square}$ $\frac{4}{3} = \square\frac{\square}{\square}$

$\frac{7}{4} = \square\frac{\square}{\square}$ $\frac{17}{12} = \square\frac{\square}{\square}$

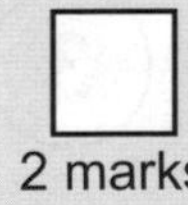
2 marks

3 What is $1\frac{4}{9}$ as an improper fraction?

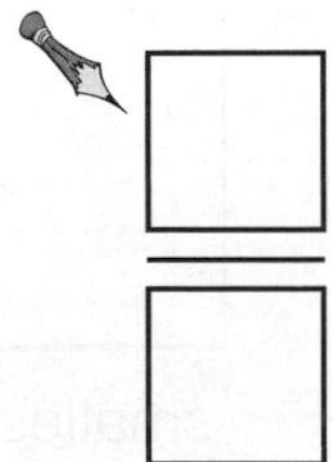

1 mark

4 What is $\frac{2}{3} + \frac{1}{6} - \frac{1}{4}$?

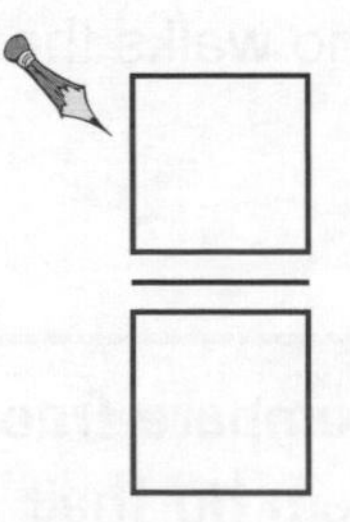

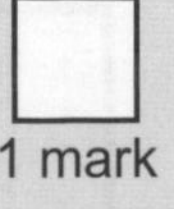
1 mark

Adding and Subtracting Fractions

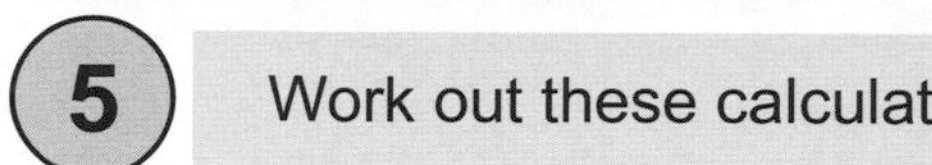

5 Work out these calculations.

Write each answer as an improper fraction and then as a mixed number.

$\frac{5}{7} + \frac{6}{7} = \frac{\square}{\square} = \square\frac{\square}{\square}$

1 mark

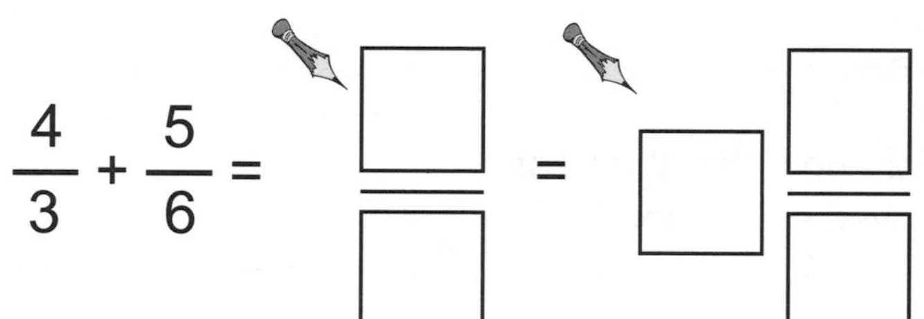

$\frac{4}{3} + \frac{5}{6} = \frac{\square}{\square} = \square\frac{\square}{\square}$

1 mark

6 Taylor has some packs of stickers. There are six stickers in each pack.

He gives each of his friends a sticker and has fourteen stickers left over. Write the number of packs he has left as a mixed number.

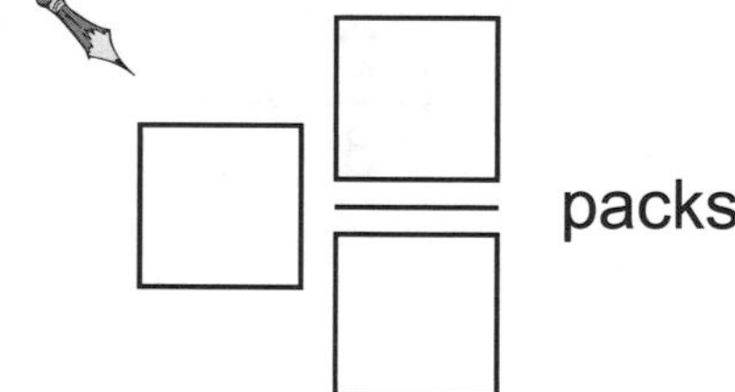

$\square\frac{\square}{\square}$ packs

1 mark

7 Andrew, James and Jenny share a box of chocolates.

Andrew eats $\frac{1}{3}$ of the chocolates, James eats $\frac{2}{5}$ and Jenny eats $\frac{1}{10}$.

What fraction of the box is left?

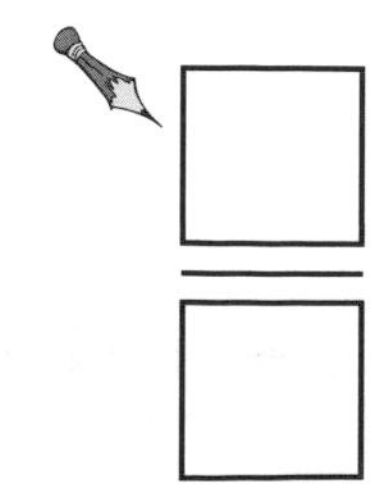

1 mark

"I can swap between mixed numbers and improper fractions. I can add and subtract fractions by finding a common denominator."

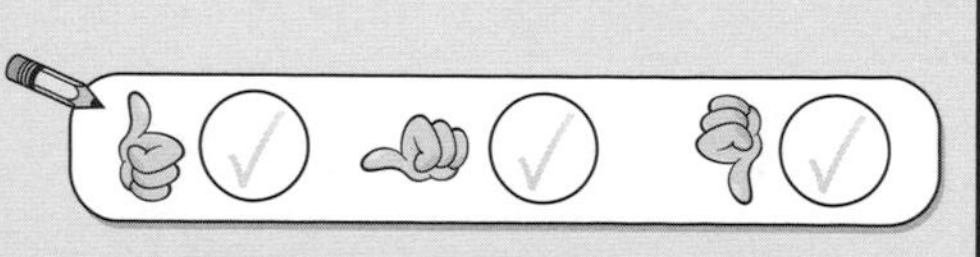

Multiplying with Fractions

1 Work out:

$\frac{1}{2} \times 4$

$\frac{2}{3} \times 12$

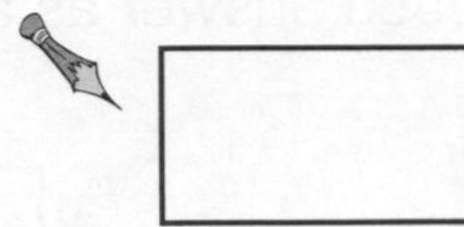

$\frac{3}{4} \times 8$

$\frac{4}{5} \times 15$

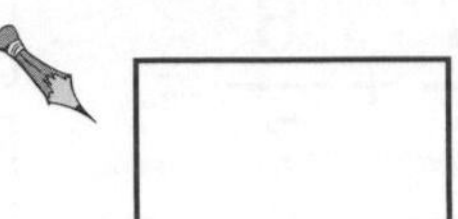

2 marks

2 There are 52 weeks in a year.

Ben has lived in London for two fifths of a year.
How many weeks has he lived in London?

weeks

1 mark

3 Calculate:

$1\frac{2}{3} \times 9$

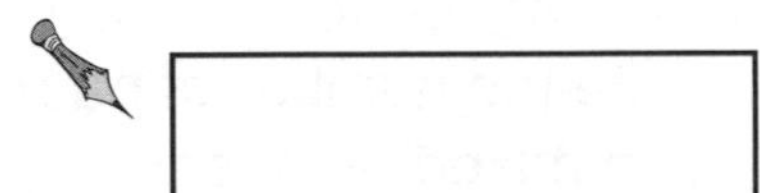

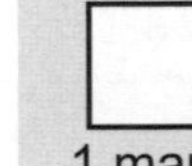

1 mark

$3\frac{1}{4} \times 8$

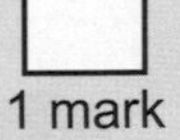

1 mark

$2\frac{3}{5} \times 10$

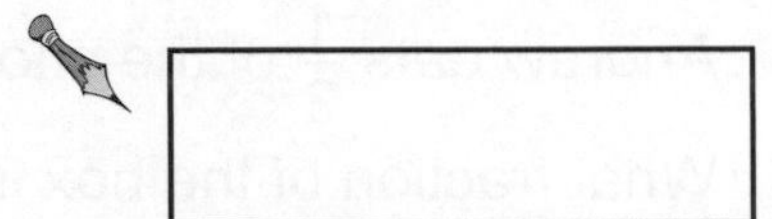

1 mark

4 Jess is baking pies for 24 people. She makes $1\frac{1}{6}$ pies for each person.

How many pies is Jess baking?

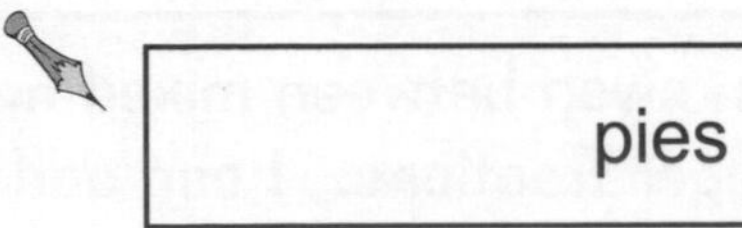

pies

1 mark

Multiplying with Fractions

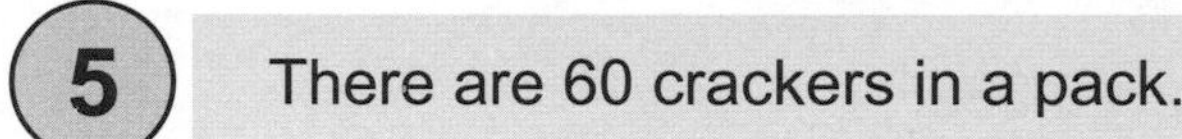

5 There are 60 crackers in a pack.

Joseph eats $2\frac{5}{12}$ packs of crackers. How many crackers does he eat?

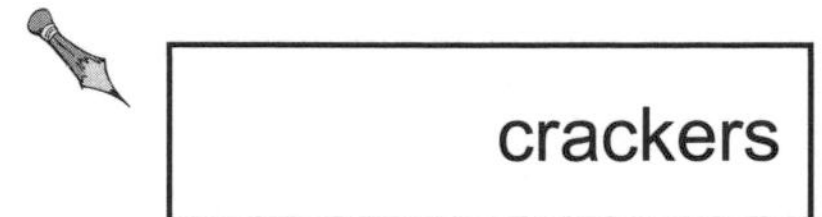

1 mark

6 Write the answers to these calculations as mixed numbers.

$2\frac{1}{6} \times 20$

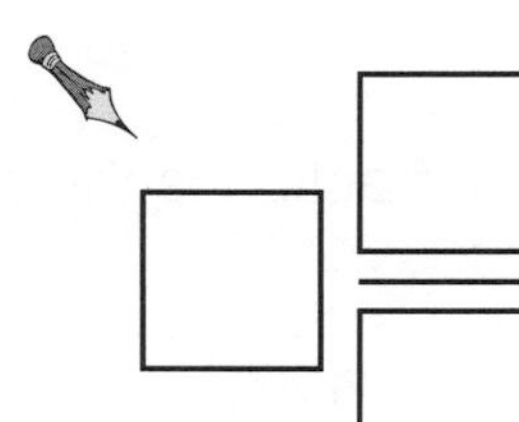

1 mark

$5\frac{2}{7} \times 12$

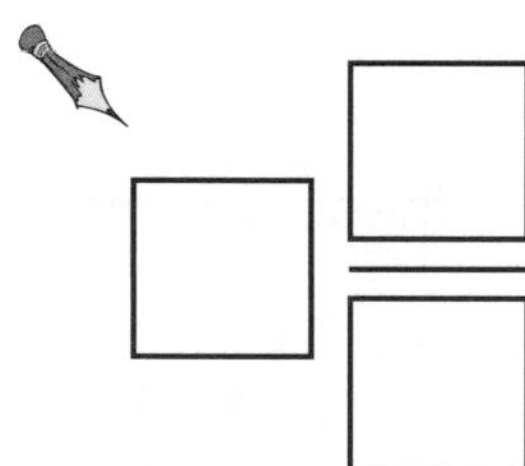

1 mark

7 Lucy has 42 sweets.

She gives $\frac{1}{6}$ of the sweets to each of her friends and has 14 sweets left over.

How many friends does Lucy have?

1 mark

8 Fill in the missing digits.

$\frac{5}{7} \times \square = 15$ $\frac{2}{9} \times \square = 6$

2 marks

"I can multiply proper fractions and mixed numbers by whole numbers."

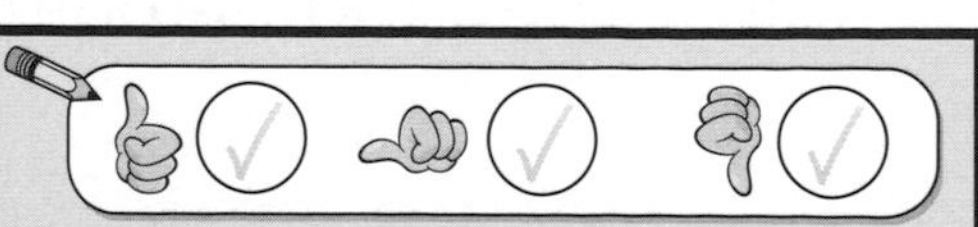

Writing Decimals as Fractions

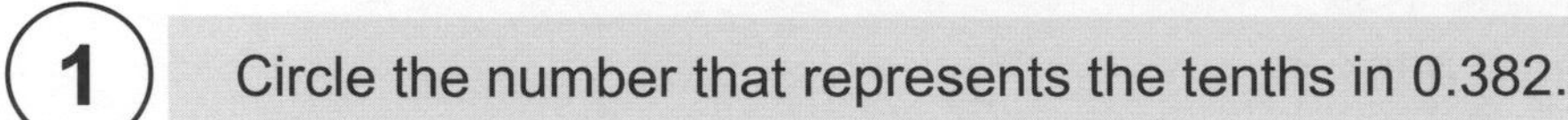

1 Circle the number that represents the tenths in 0.382.

0 3 8 2

1 mark

2 What is the value of the digit '1' in 0.51?

1 mark

3 Which fraction is the same as 0.014? Circle your answer.

$\frac{140}{1000}$ $\frac{14}{100}$ $\frac{4}{10}$ $\frac{140}{100}$ $\frac{14}{1000}$

1 mark

4 Write these decimals as fractions.

$0.9 = \frac{\square}{\square}$ $0.253 = \frac{\square}{\square}$

2 marks

5 Write the following as fractions:

nine tenths

1 mark

twenty hundredths

1 mark

thirty three thousandths

1 mark

Writing Decimals as Fractions

6 Match each decimal to its equivalent fraction.

One of them has been done for you.

1.3 0.07 0.59 0.4 5.9 0.5

$\frac{5}{10}$ $\frac{59}{10}$ $\frac{13}{10}$ $\frac{59}{100}$ $\frac{4}{10}$ $\frac{7}{100}$

2 marks

7 Write these fractions as decimals.

$\frac{3}{10}$  

$\frac{27}{100}$ 

$\frac{9}{100}$  

$\frac{312}{1000}$ 

2 marks

8 Write these decimals as mixed numbers.

The first one has been done for you.

1.31 = $1\frac{31}{100}$

6.7 =

2.06 =

8.14 =

20.6 =

15.081 =

2 marks

"I can read and write decimals as fractions."

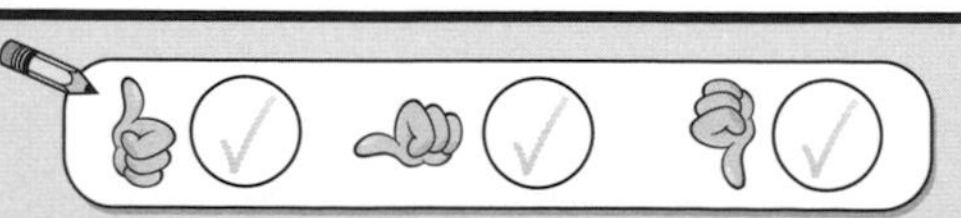

Rounding Decimals

1 Round each of these decimals to the nearest whole number.

0.98 ☐ 6.49 ☐

13.73 ☐ 9.19 ☐

2 marks

2 What is 27.47 rounded to the nearest whole number?

☐

1 mark

3 Round these decimals to one decimal place.

8.74 ☐ 29.35 ☐

14.09 ☐ 1.81 ☐

2 marks

4 Martin lives 16.55 km from the beach.

Round the distance from Martin's house to the beach to one decimal place.

☐ km

1 mark

Rounding Decimals

5 Round these weights to one decimal place.

31.61 kg | 2.25 kg | 23.29 g

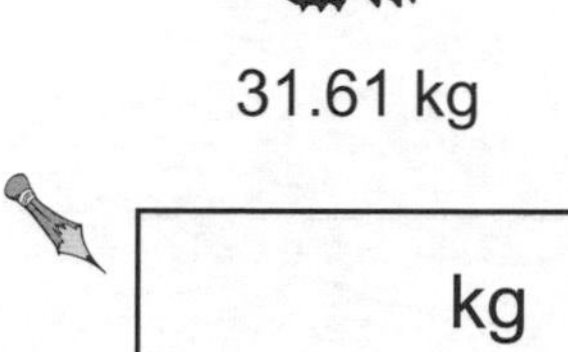

kg

kg

g

1 mark

6 Kirsty's house is 7.63 m tall. What is its height:

to the nearest metre?

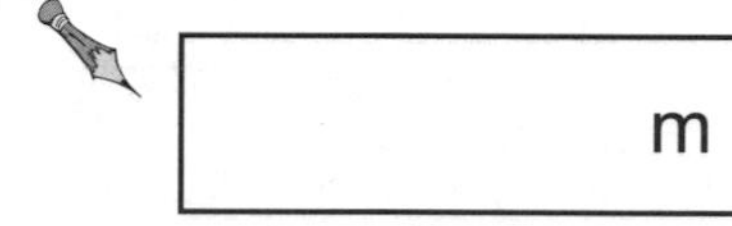

m

1 mark

to 1 decimal place?

m

1 mark

7 Estimate the answers to these calculations by rounding these decimals to whole numbers.

2.65 × 7.13

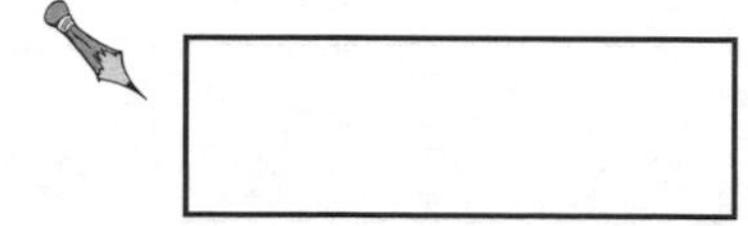

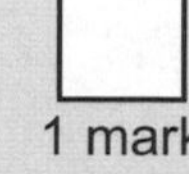

1 mark

64.05 – 29.80

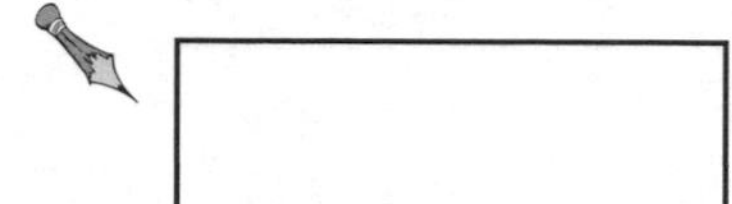

1 mark

8 Circle the number that is closest to 4.

3.89   4.08   3.9   4.97   4.2   3.09

1 mark

"I can round decimals with two decimal places to the nearest whole number or to one decimal place."

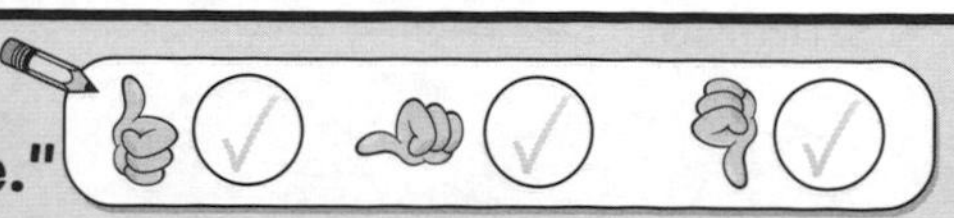

Ordering and Comparing Decimals

1 Circle the smaller number in each pair.

4.10 or 4.06

1 mark

1.274 or 1.391

1 mark

9.173 or 9.602

1 mark

0.165 or 0.150

1 mark

2 Paul is 1.72 m tall, Trisha is 1.58 m tall, Ash is 1.55 m tall, Sophie is 1.38 m tall and Ben is 1.76 m tall.

Who is the tallest?

1 mark

Who is the shortest?

1 mark

3 Put these decimals into order from smallest to largest.

1.975 2.180 1.505 1.925 2.035

smallest → largest

1 mark

Ordering and Comparing Decimals

4 Put these decimals into order from largest to smallest.

0.392   0.908   0.397   0.484   0.918

largest → smallest

1 mark

5 Circle the smallest number below.

0.58   0.05   0.8   0.085   5.08

1 mark

6 Put these decimals into order from smallest to largest.

0.285   0.28   0.297   0.2   0.027

smallest → largest

1 mark

7 Put these weights in order from heaviest to lightest.

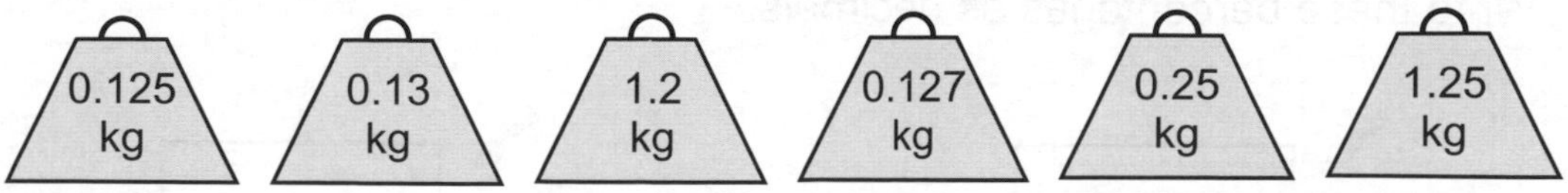

0.125 kg   0.13 kg   1.2 kg   0.127 kg   0.25 kg   1.25 kg

1 mark

"I can read, write, compare and solve problems with numbers with up to 3 decimal places."

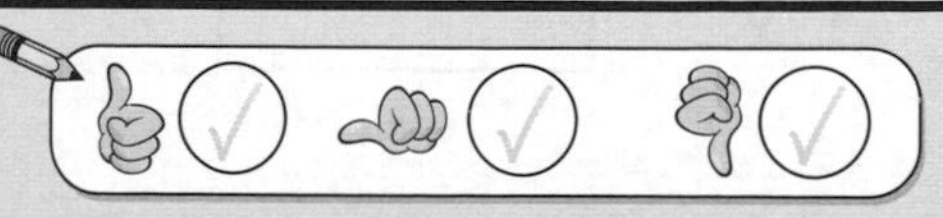

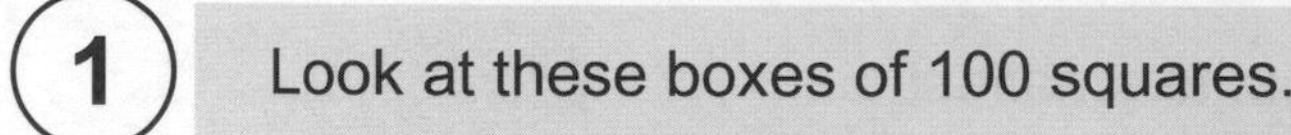

Percentages

1 Look at these boxes of 100 squares.

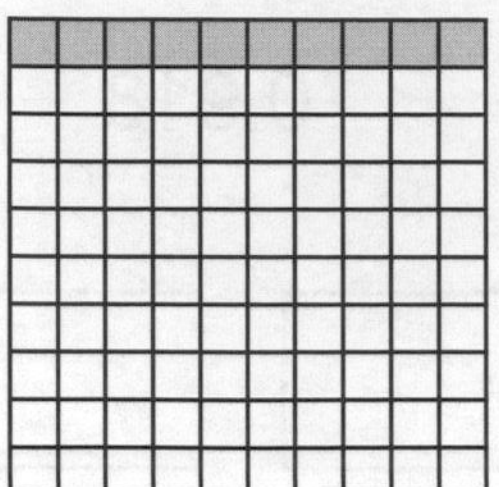

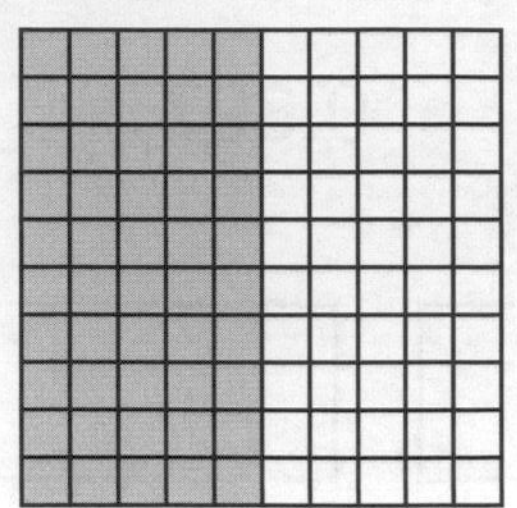

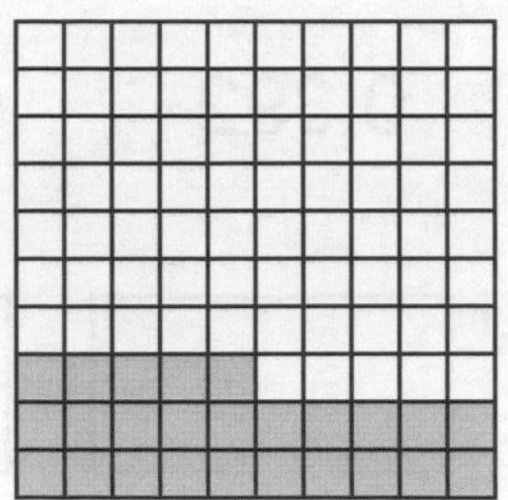

What percentage of each box is shaded?

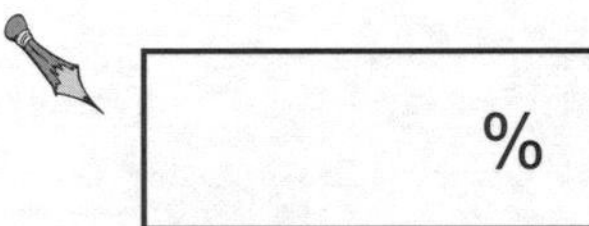

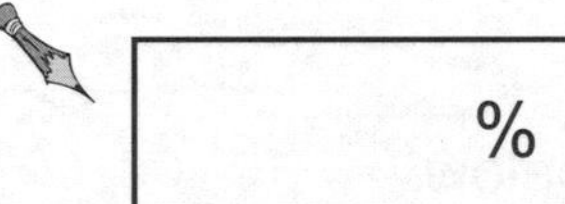

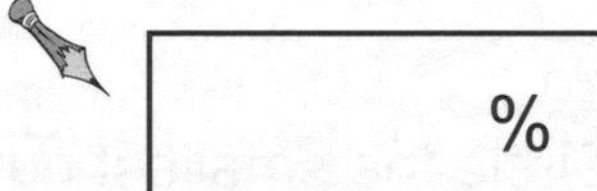

3 marks

2 In a spelling test, Alex got 83% of the words right.

What percentage of the words did he get wrong?

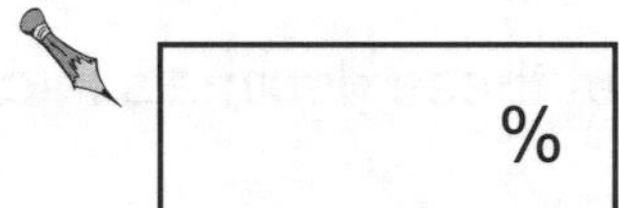

3 Write these fractions as percentages.

$\frac{85}{100}$ [   ] %

$\frac{3}{10}$ [   ] %

2 marks

4 Write these percentages as decimals.

60% = [   ]

43% = [   ]

4% = [   ]

80% = [   ]

2 marks

Percentages

5 Circle the percentage of each shape that is shaded.

The first one has been done for you.

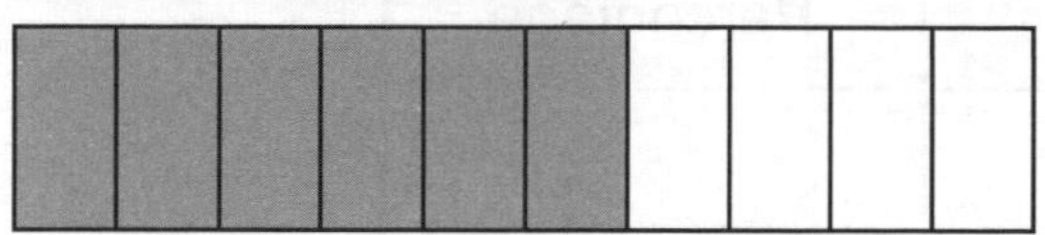

40%	50%
~~60%~~ (circled) 60%	4%

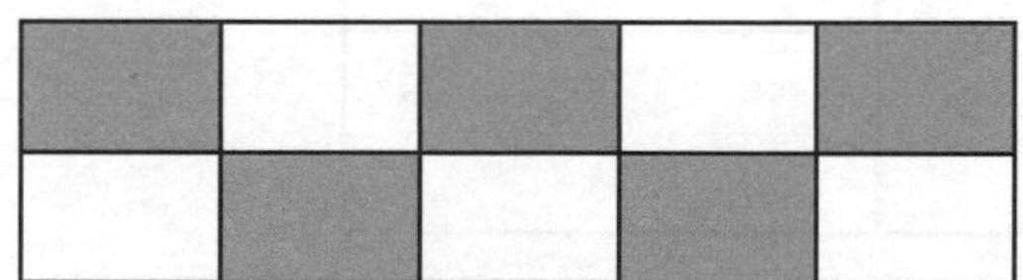

5%	25%
10%	50%

1 mark

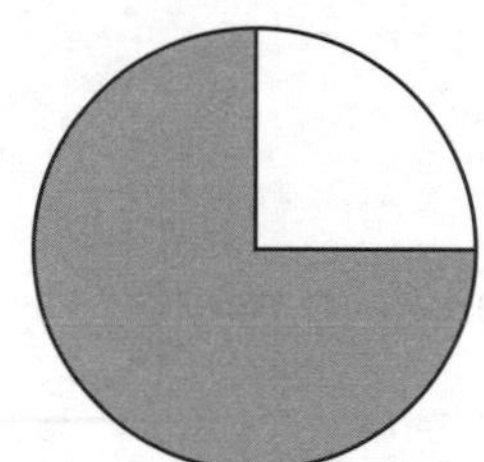

85%	75%
25%	55%

1 mark

6 Fill in the missing numbers.

$50\% = \frac{\square}{100} = \frac{\square}{2}$ $10\% = \frac{\square}{100} = \frac{1}{\square}$

2 marks

7 Rita asked her classmates to vote for their favourite school subject.

$\frac{4}{10}$ of her classmates voted for maths and 26% voted for music.
Which subject got more votes?

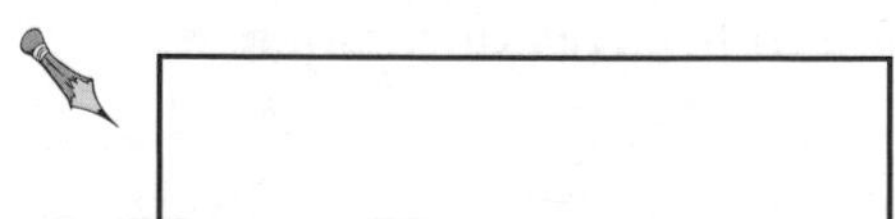

1 mark

"I know what % means and I can write percentages as fractions or decimals."

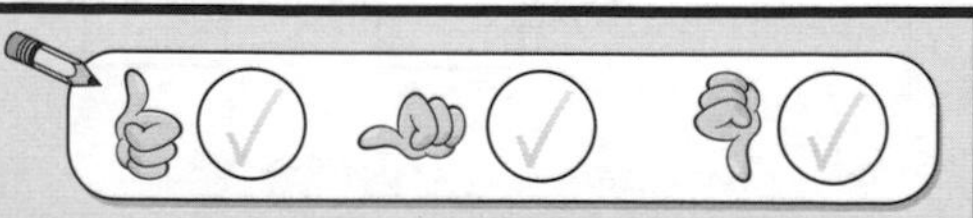

Fraction, Decimal and Percentage Problems

1 Complete this table.

Give all fractions with the smallest possible denominator.

Fraction	Decimal	Percentage
	0.5	
		60%
$\frac{3}{4}$		

2 marks

2 Shayla is reading a book. She has read $\frac{2}{5}$ so far.

What percentage of the book does Shayla have left to read?

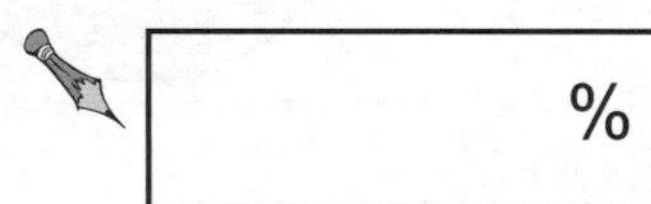
%

1 mark

3 $\frac{4}{25}$ of sheep in Oakshire are brown.

Write the number of brown sheep as a decimal.

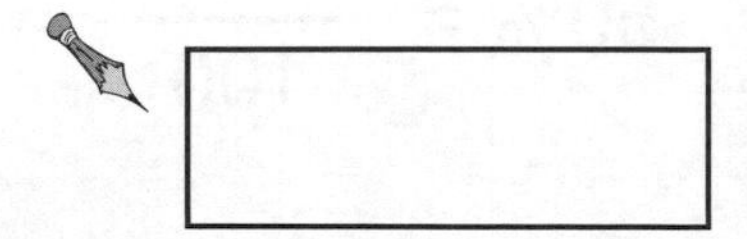

1 mark

12% of sheep in Birchwall are brown.
Which county has the larger percentage of brown sheep?

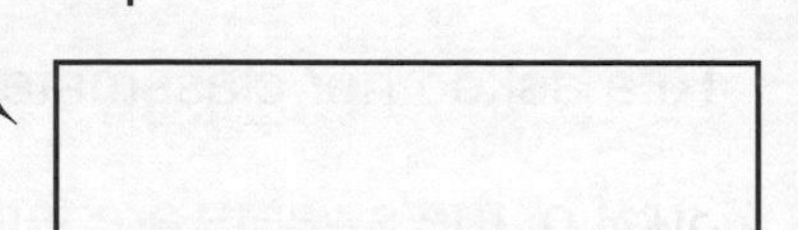

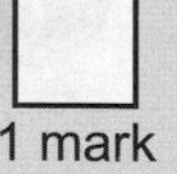
1 mark

4 Fill in the missing digits.

4.6 ☐ 5 + ☐ .21 = 7.81 ☐

1 mark

Fraction, Decimal and Percentage Problems

5 Richard and Matthew own a computer game.
Richard has finished $\frac{3}{4}$ of it. Matthew has finished $\frac{8}{10}$.

How much more of the game has Matthew finished than Richard?
Give your answer as a percentage. Show your working.

%

2 marks

6 Farmer Fred has 200 sheep on his farm.

He sells 40 of them. What percentage of his sheep does he have left?

%

1 mark

7 Rhys has £120. He buys a scooter for £26.65 and a hat for £3.35.

How much does he spend altogether?

£

1 mark

What percentage of his money does he spend?

%

1 mark

8 There are 300 sweets in a pack.

30% of the sweets are lemon flavour, $\frac{1}{5}$ are strawberry flavour and the rest are orange flavour.
How many orange flavour sweets are there?

sweets

2 marks

"I can convert fractions into percentages and decimals. I can solve problems that involve fractions, decimals and percentages."

Metric Units

1 Convert these lengths:

2.9 cm into mm.

mm

700 cm into m.

m

2 marks

2 Convert these measurements:

3.7 litres into millilitres.

ml

2700 g into kg.

kg

2 marks

3 Valerie's lizard has a weight of 0.2 kg. It is 0.3 m long.

What is the lizard's weight in grams?

g

1 mark

How long is the lizard in cm?

cm

1 mark

4 A pigeon's wing is 0.35 m long.
An eagle's wing is 1.7 m longer.

How long is an eagle's wing?
Give your answer in cm.

cm

1 mark

5 What is 5 km in cm?

cm

1 mark

Metric Units

6 Andy has a jug with a capacity of 2 litres.

He puts 0.6 litres of juice into the jug.
He fills the rest of the jug with lemonade.
How many millilitres of lemonade does Andy put into the jug?

ml

1 mark

7 Lana has used a tenth of her half kilogram bag of flour.

How much has she used in grams?

g

1 mark

8 Jen buys two sacks of potatoes.
Sack A has a mass of 1005 g and Sack B has a mass of 1.2 kg.

What is the difference in mass of the two sacks?
Give your answer in grams.

g

1 mark

9 Sarah takes her dog for an 800 m walk three times a week.

How far will she have walked with her dog after two weeks?
Give your answer in km.

km

1 mark

"I can convert between different units."

Imperial Units

1 Convert these measurements:

3 metres into feet.

feet

5 kilograms into pounds.

pounds

2 marks

2 Circle the largest measurement in each pair.

8 inches or 22 cm

9 kilograms or 4 pounds

400 grams or 40 ounces

15 miles or 10 kilometres

2 marks

3 This scale shows how to convert between kilograms and ounces.

kilograms 0 0.1 0.2 0.3

ounces 0 4 8 12

Approximately how many ounces is 200 g?

ounces

1 mark

Use your answer to work out approximately how many ounces are in 1 kg.

ounces

1 mark

Imperial Units

4 Bob cycles 24 km twice a week.

How many miles does he cycle in total every week?

miles

1 mark

5 Geraldine is making a cake. The recipe says she needs 1.5 pints of milk. She has a one litre bottle.

Will she have enough milk?

1 mark

The recipe also says that Geraldine needs 15 ounces of flour.
She has 500 g of flour in her cupboard.

How much flour will be left over? Give your answer in ounces.

ounces

1 mark

6 Convert 5 miles into feet.

feet

1 mark

"I can convert roughly between imperial and metric units."

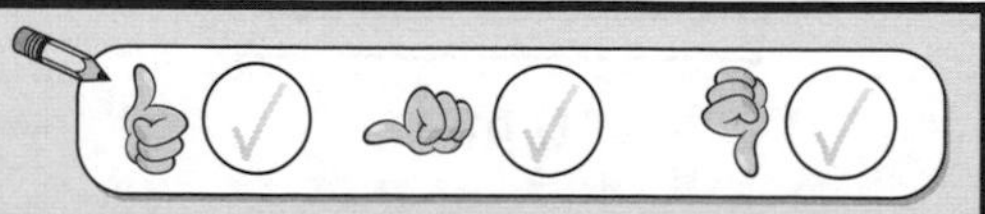

Perimeter

1. Calculate the perimeters of the shapes below.

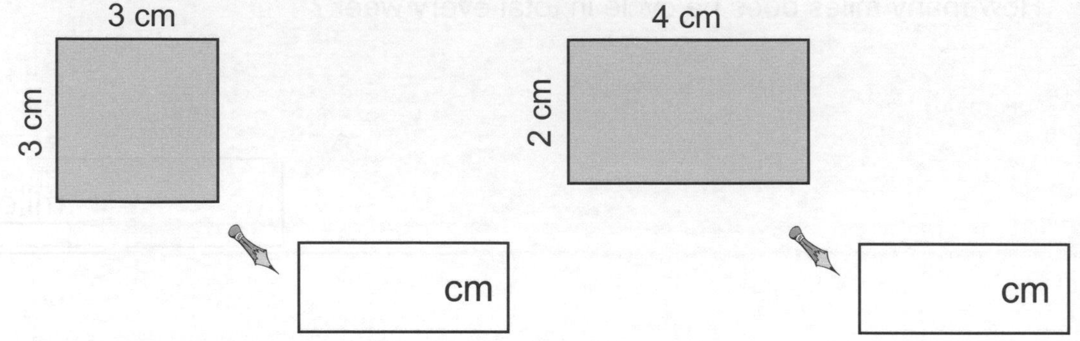

2 marks

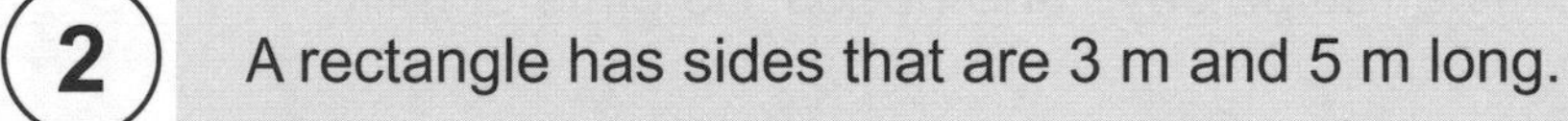

2. A rectangle has sides that are 3 m and 5 m long.

Work out its perimeter.

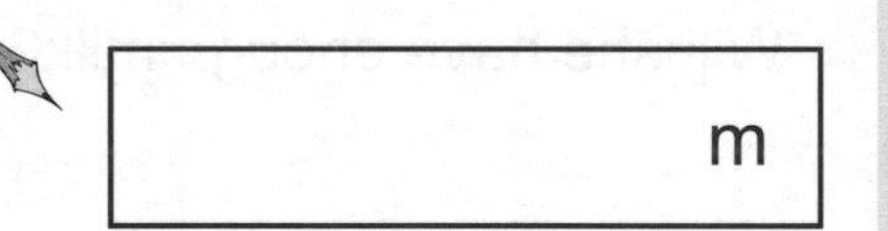

1 mark

3. The shape below is made up of 3 identical squares.

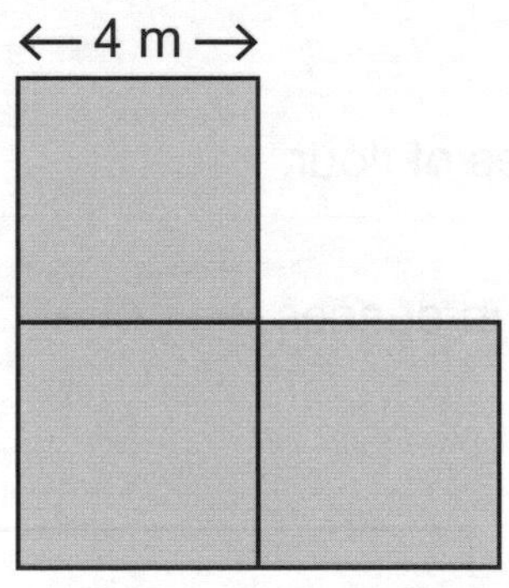

Find its perimeter.

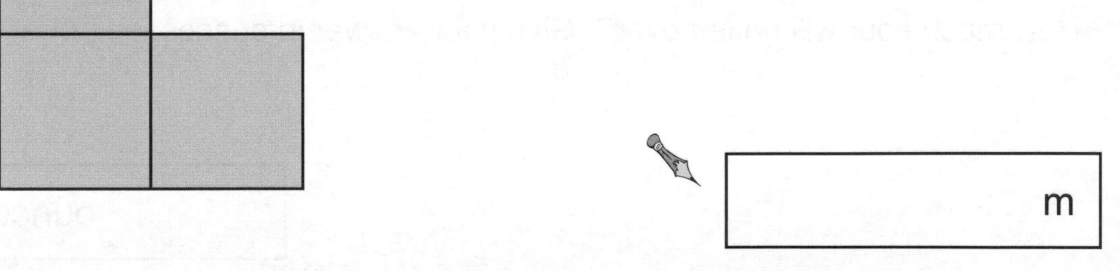

1 mark

4. Calculate the perimeter of this shape.
The diagram has not been drawn to scale.

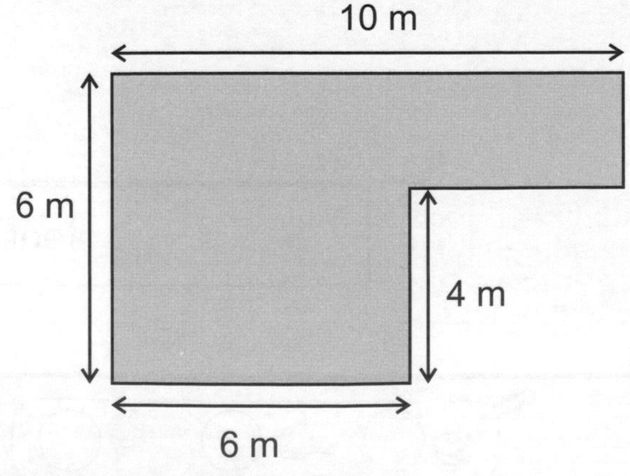

m

1 mark

Perimeter

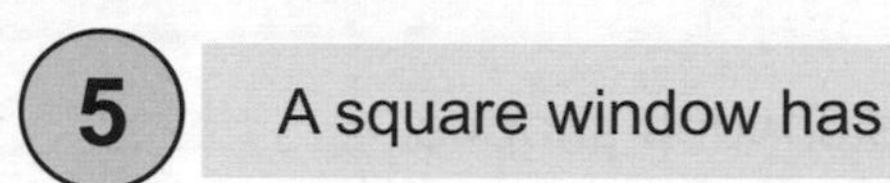

5 A square window has a perimeter of 16 cm.

How long is each side of the window?

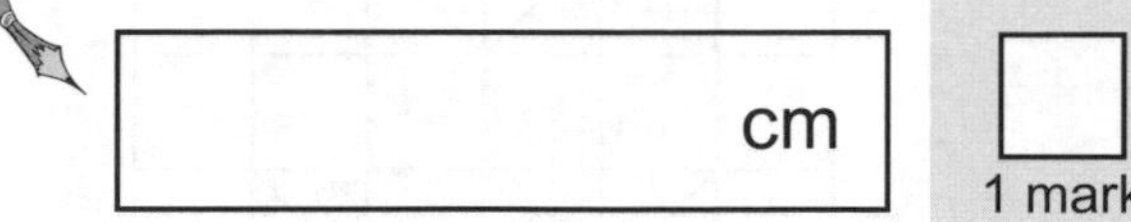

1 mark

6 Dave has three identical rectangular tiles.
He makes this shape from the tiles.

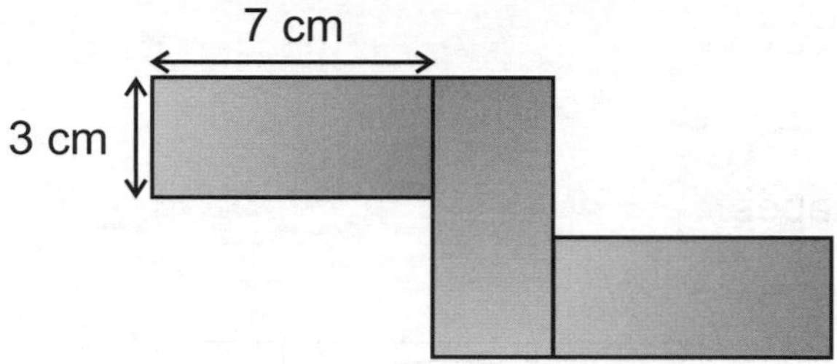

Find the perimeter of the shape.

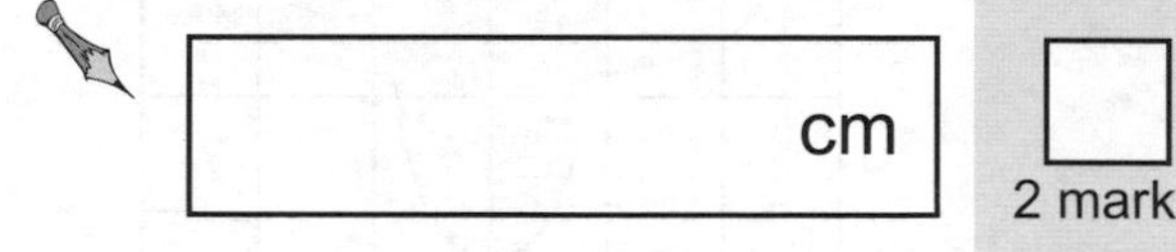

2 marks

7 A rectangle has a length of 8 m and a perimeter of 22 m.

Find the width of the rectangle.

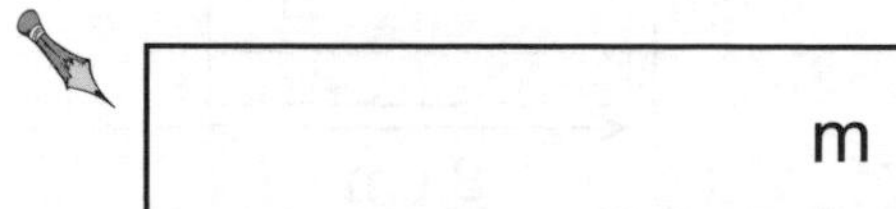

2 marks

"I can measure and calculate the perimeters of shapes."

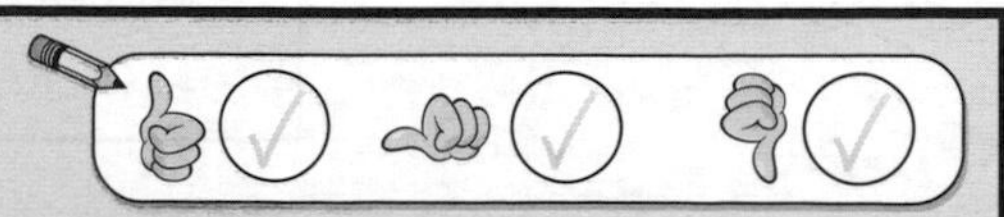

Area

1 Each square on the grids is 1 m^2. Find the areas of the shaded shapes.

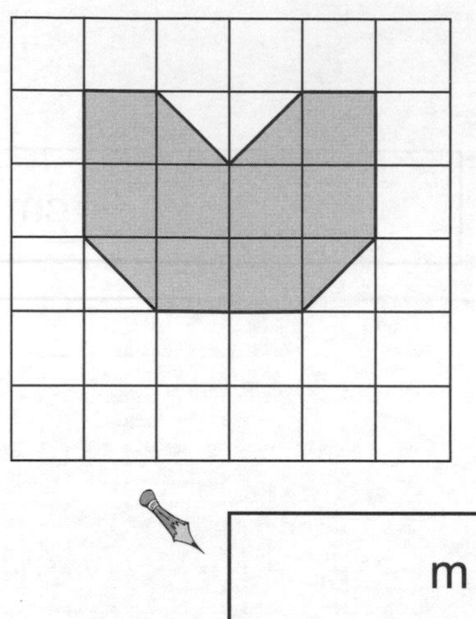

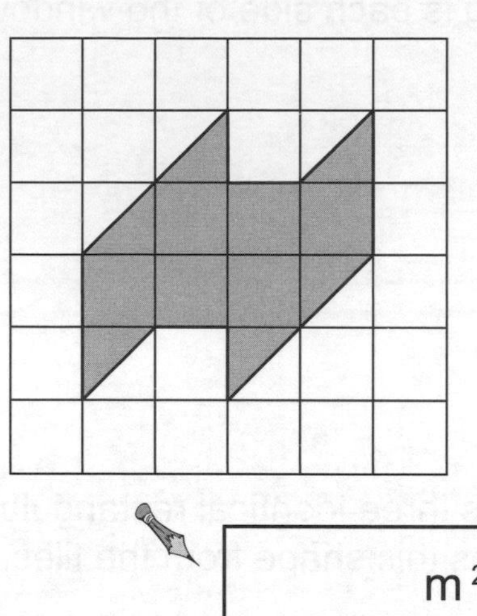

m^2 m^2

2 marks

2 Each square on the grids is 1 cm^2.
Estimate the areas of the shaded shapes.

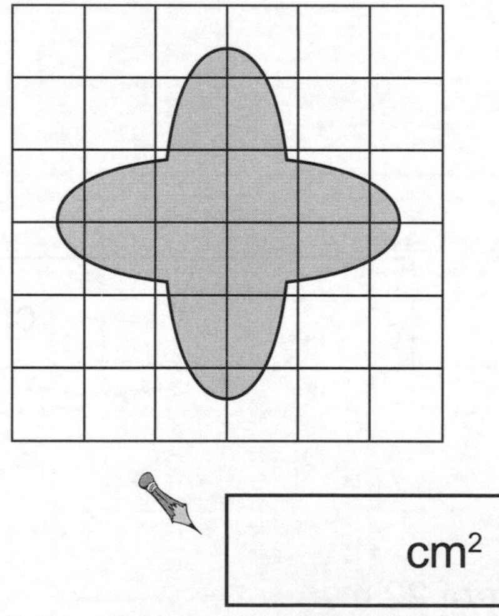

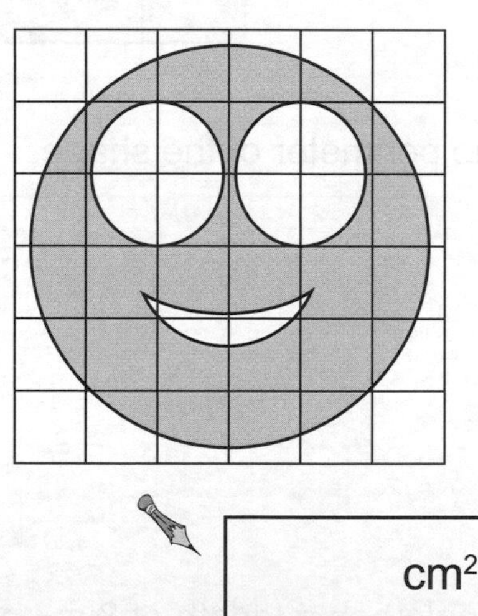

cm^2 cm^2

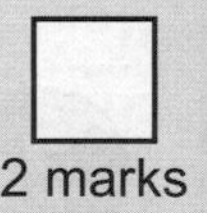

2 marks

3 Work out the areas of the shapes below.

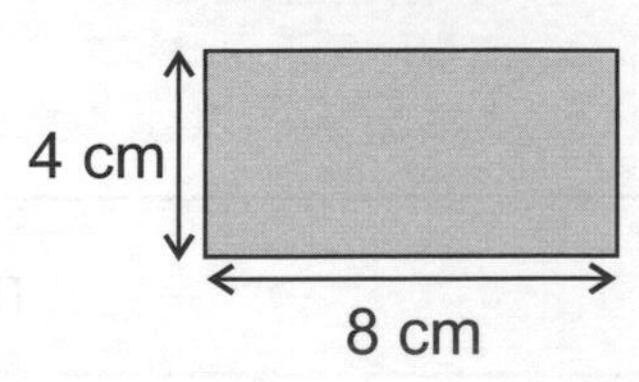

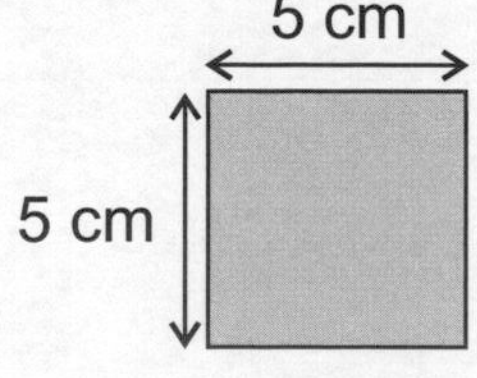

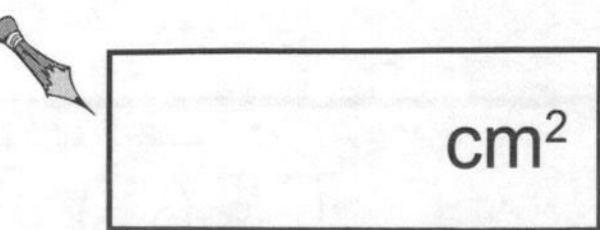

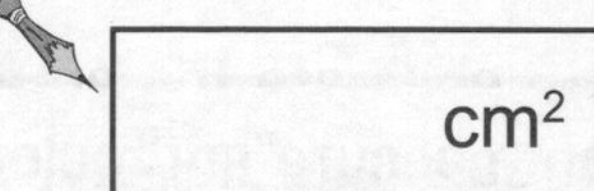

2 marks

Area

4 Here is a rectangle.

A B C D

Use a ruler to accurately measure:

The rectangle's length from A to B. cm

The rectangle's width from B to C. cm

1 mark

Calculate the area of the rectangle.
Show your working.

cm^2

1 mark

5 Amrit is putting a new carpet in his bedroom.
The room measures 9 m by 8 m.

How many square metres of carpet will Amrit need?

m^2

1 mark

6 A rectangular garden has an area of 56 m^2.
Its length is 8 m. What is its width?

m

1 mark

**"I can estimate the area of irregular shapes.
I can calculate the area of squares and rectangles and use units like cm^2 and m^2."**

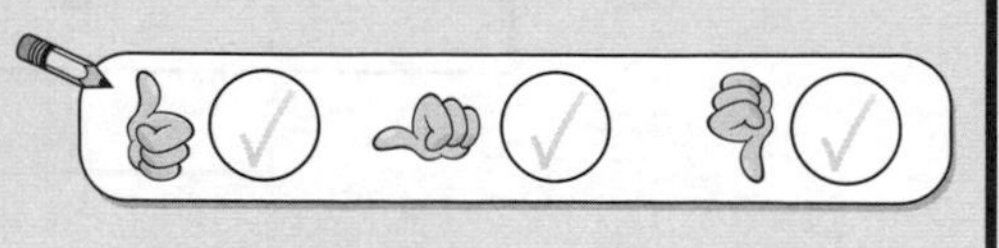

Estimating Volume and Capacity

1 Each cube has a volume of 1 cm^3.
Work out the volume of each of these shapes.

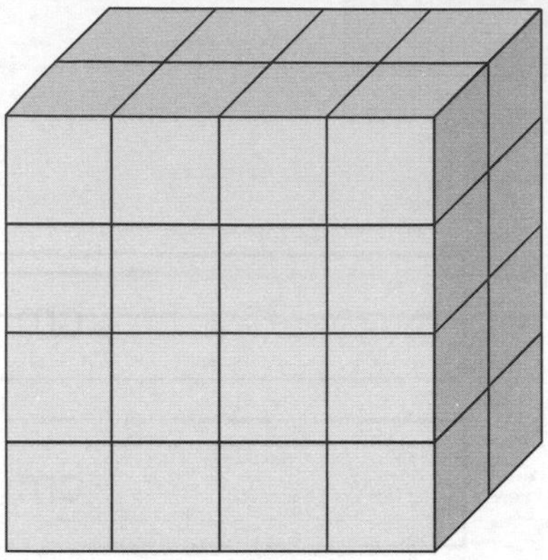

cm^3

1 mark

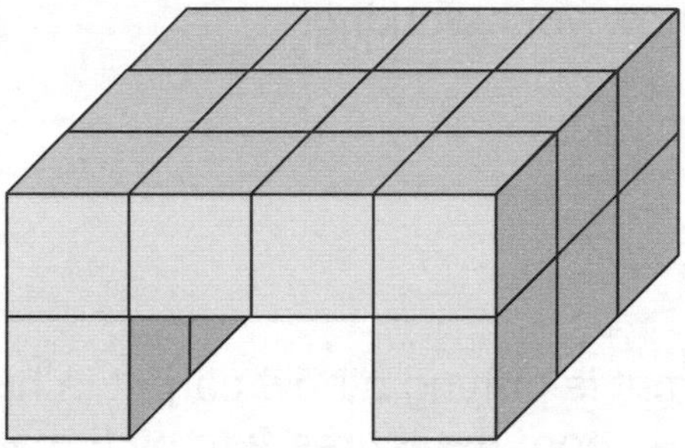

cm^3

1 mark

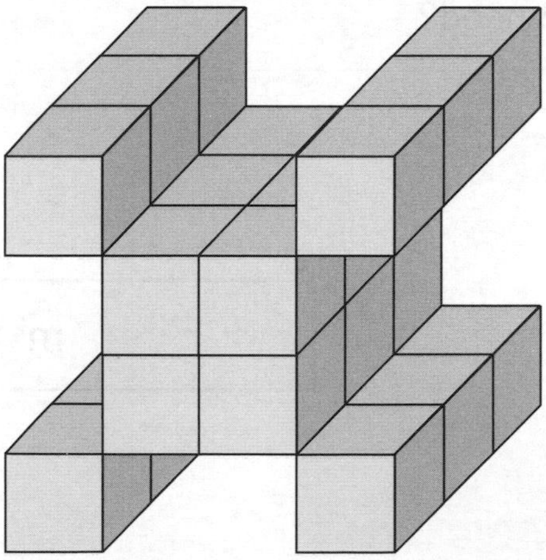

cm^3

1 mark

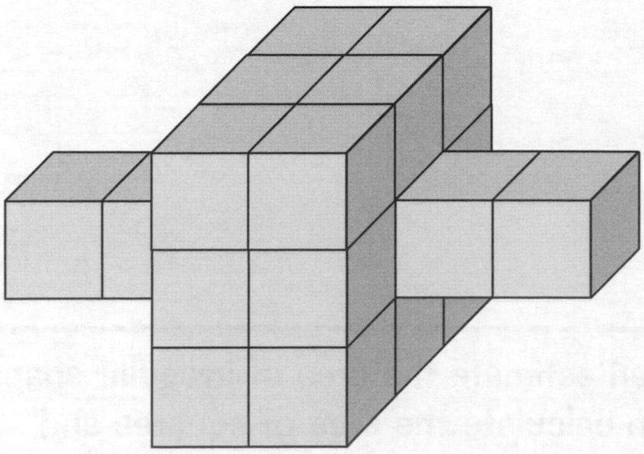

cm^3

1 mark

Estimating Volume and Capacity

Luke has made this shape out of cubes. Each cube has a volume of 1 cm^3.

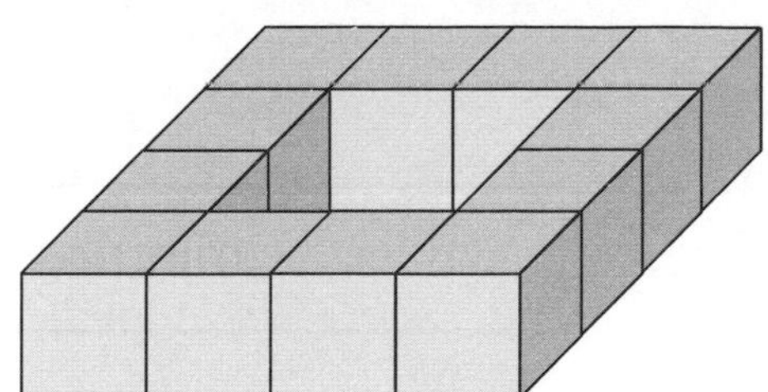

He makes the same shape 5 more times and stacks them on top of each other.

What is the volume of the stack?

cm^3

1 mark

The stack has a hole through the centre.
What is the capacity of the hole?

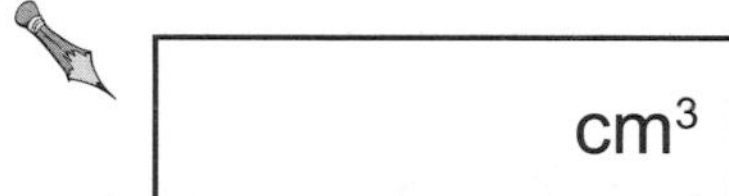

cm^3

1 mark

3 Billy makes the body of a model car by sticking centimetre cubes together, as shown on the right.

Find the volume of the car body.

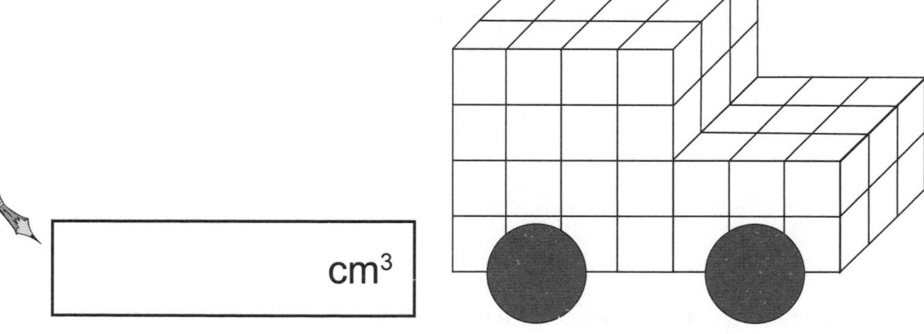

cm^3

1 mark

Billy adds a boot to the car. The new volume of the car is 78 cm^3.
If the boot is 3 cubes wide and 2 cubes long, how many cubes high is it?

cubes

1 mark

"I can estimate volume and capacity."

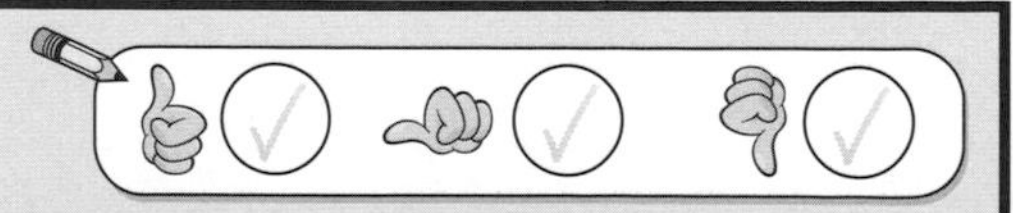

Solving Time and Measurement Problems

1 Amir's bus will be arriving in one and a half hours.

How many minutes is this?

minutes

1 mark

20 minutes before the bus arrives Amir's grandma phones him.
The phone call lasts 120 seconds.
How much time is left to catch the bus after the phonecall?

minutes

1 mark

2 Freda saves £5 every day for 4 weeks and 2 days.

How much money will she have saved?

£

1 mark

Barry saves twice as much per day as Freda.
How much will Barry have saved?

£

1 mark

3 Jack's garden is shown below. Jack has 46 m of fencing.
Is this enough to go round his garden? Show your working.

1 mark

Solving Time and Measurement Problems

4 This is a diagram of a storage container:

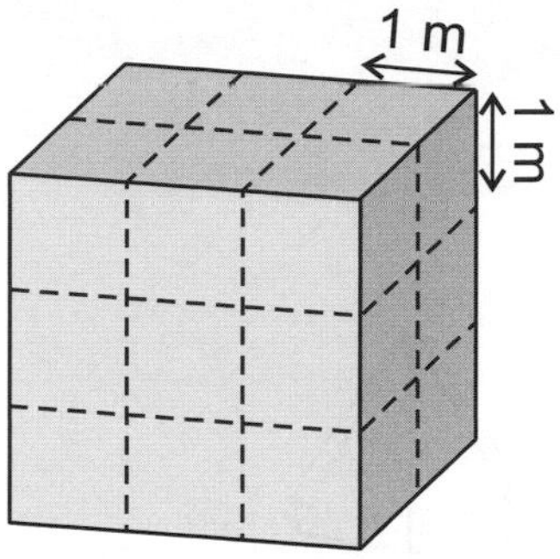

1 m

1 m

Storage containers cost £22 per m^3.
How much would it cost to buy this container?

£

1 mark

5 Jeremy and Lewis are racing their cars around a track.
The track is 10 miles long.

Jeremy's car breaks down after 14 kilometres.
Did he manage to reach the finish line?

1 mark

Lewis drives 1 mile every 40 seconds.
How long will it take him to finish the race?
Give your answer in minutes and seconds.

1 mark

6 A square tile has an area of 36 cm^2.

How many tiles would you need to put side by side so that they have a total length of 0.54 m?

tiles

1 mark

"I can solve problems that involve converting between units, and that involve money and measurements."

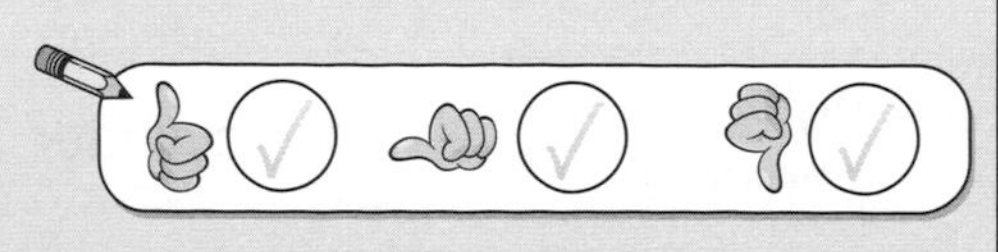

3D Shapes

1 Some 3D shapes and plan views are shown below.

Draw a line joining each 3D shape to its plan view.

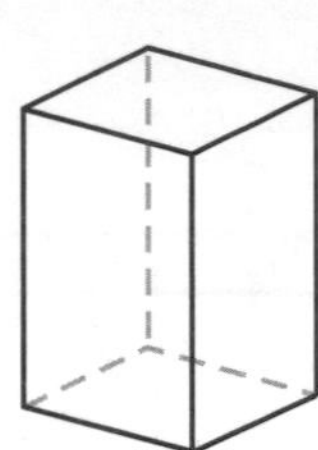
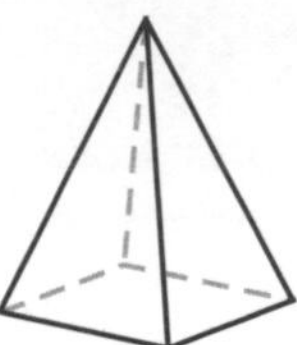
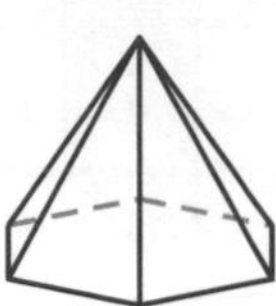

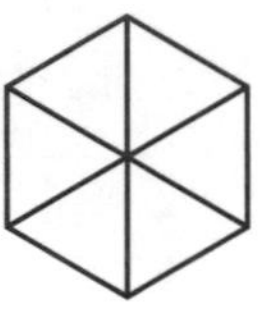
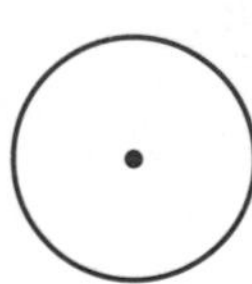

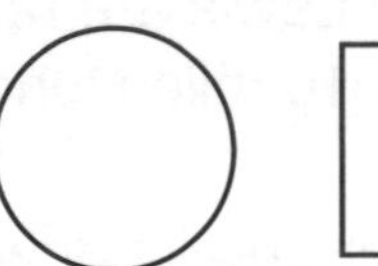

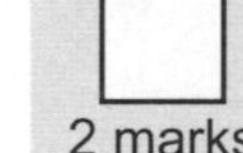
2 marks

2 Circle the nets that will fold up to make a cube.

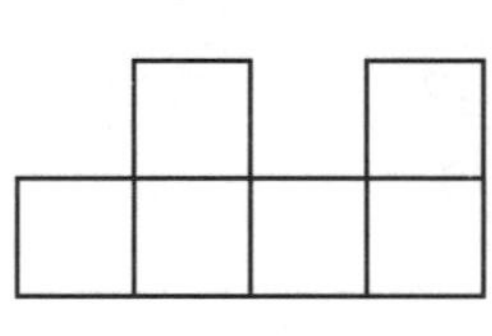
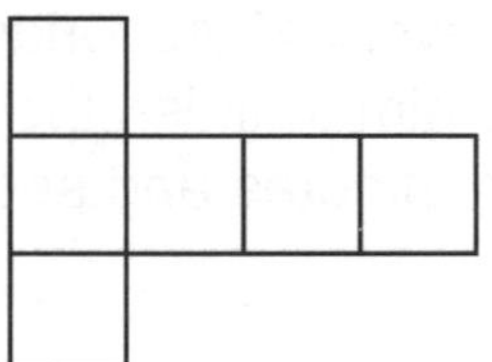
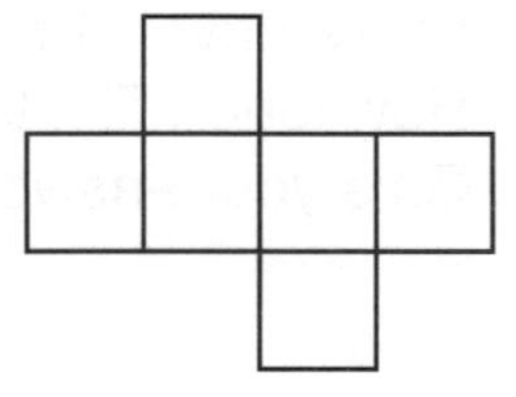

1 mark

3 Draw lines to match each net to the 3D shape it will make.

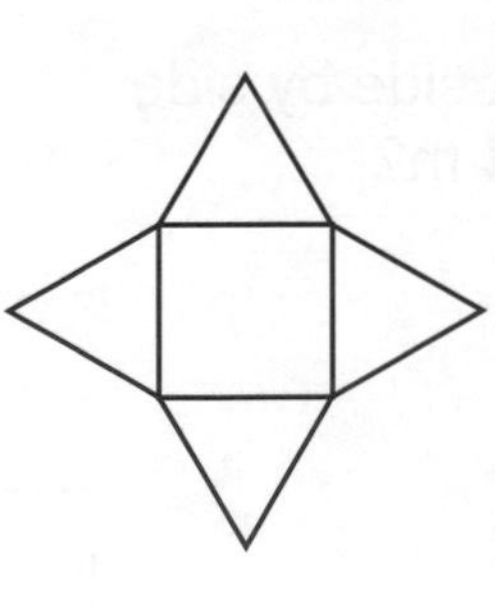
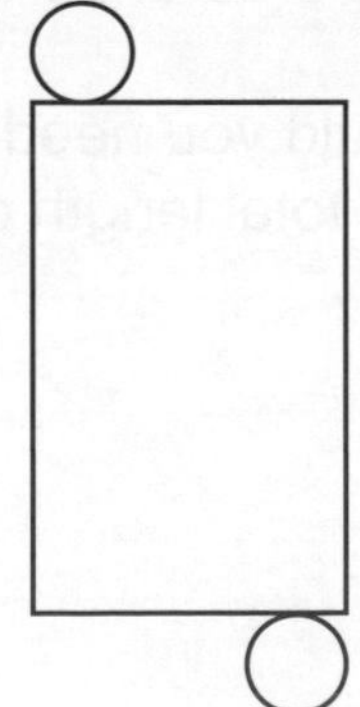
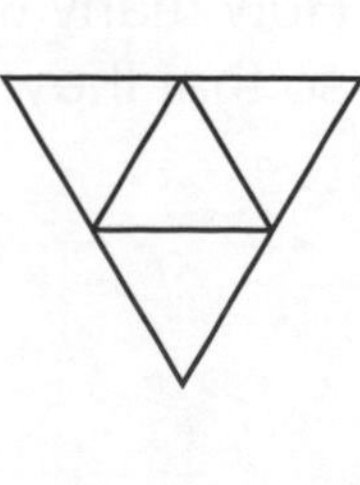

triangle-based pyramid | cylinder | square-based pyramid | triangular prism

2 marks

3D Shapes

Look at the nets below.

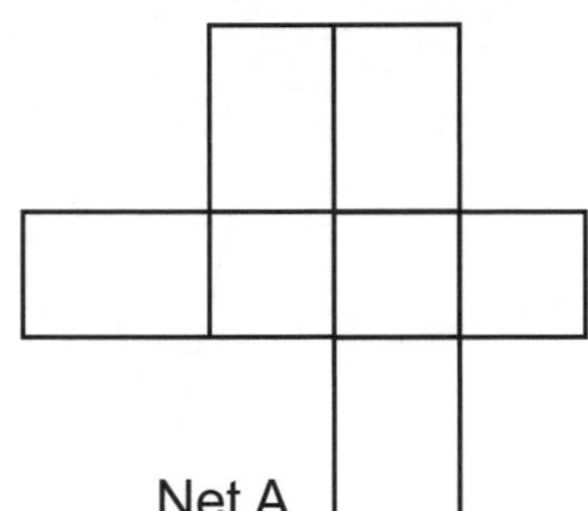

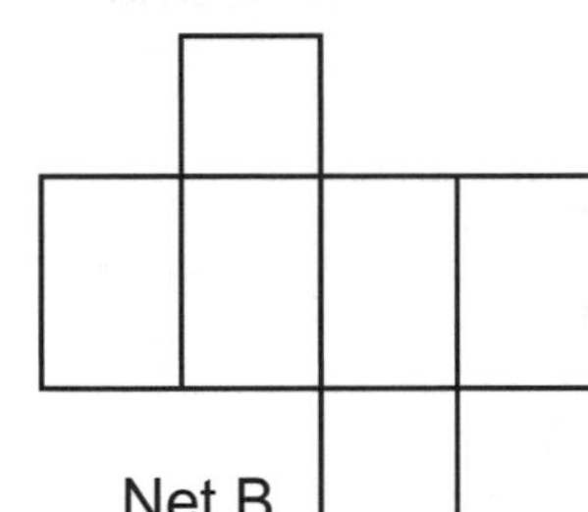

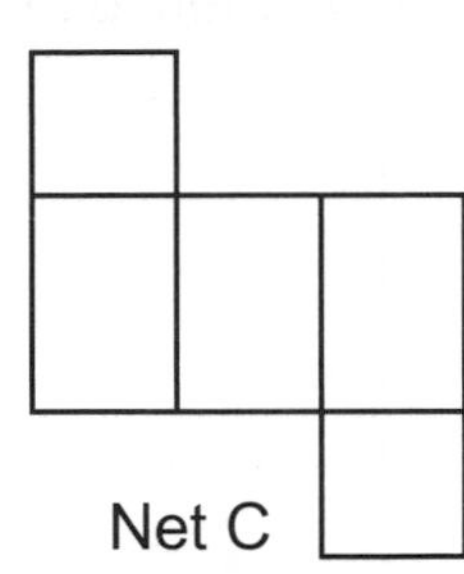

Write the letter of the net that will fold up to make a cuboid.

1 mark

5 Look at the prism below.

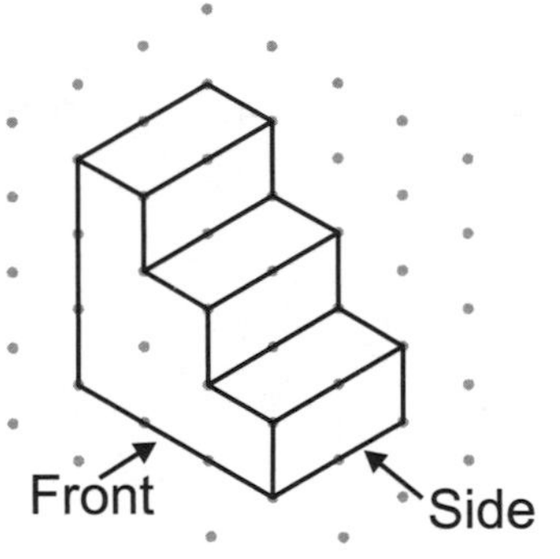

On the grid provided, draw the plan of the prism.

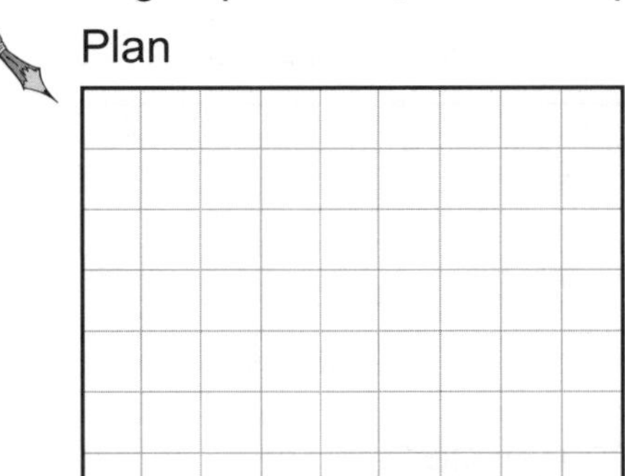

1 mark

On the grids provided, draw the front and side elevations of the prism.

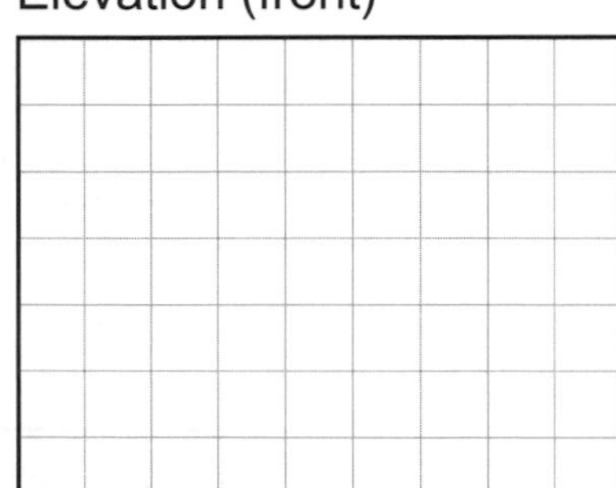

2 marks

"I can recognise 3D shapes from their nets, plans and elevations."

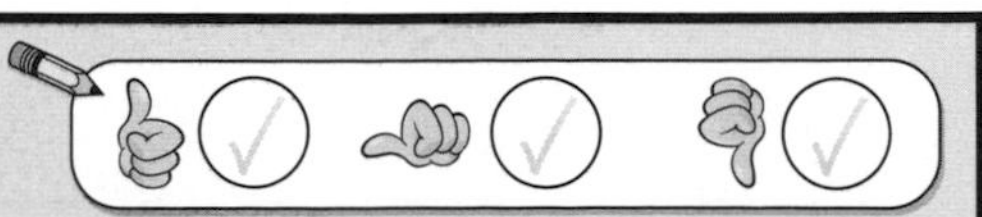

Angles

1 Look at the angles below.

Draw lines joining each angle to its name.

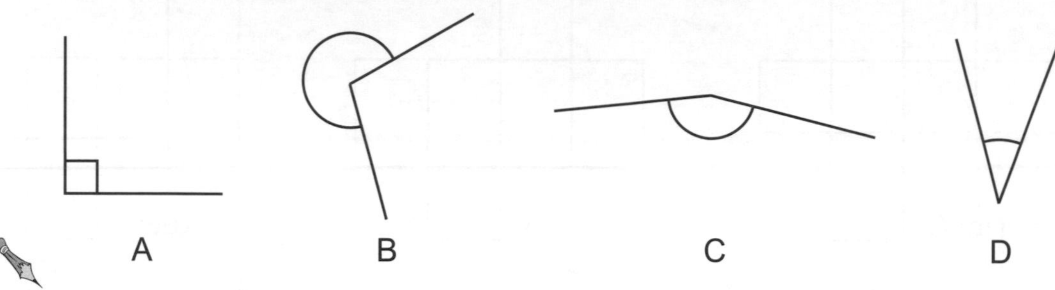

Obtuse Reflex Acute Right angle

2 marks

Place the angles in order from smallest to largest.
Write the letter of the correct angle in each box.

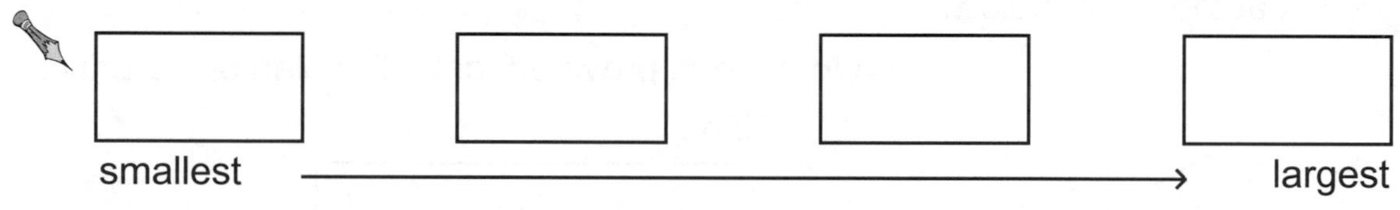

1 mark

2 Look at these three angles.

Use a protractor to measure each angle and write the answer in the box.

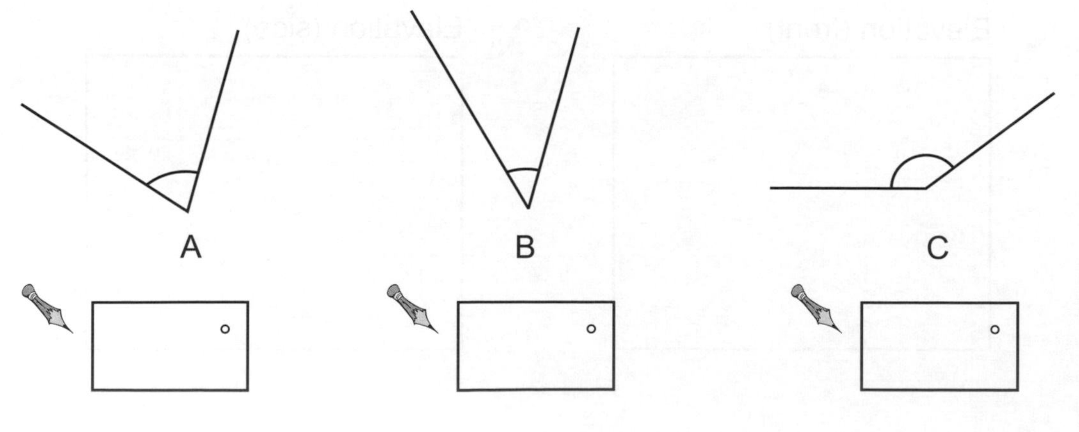

3 marks

Angles

3 Measure the acute angle in this shape. Use a protractor.

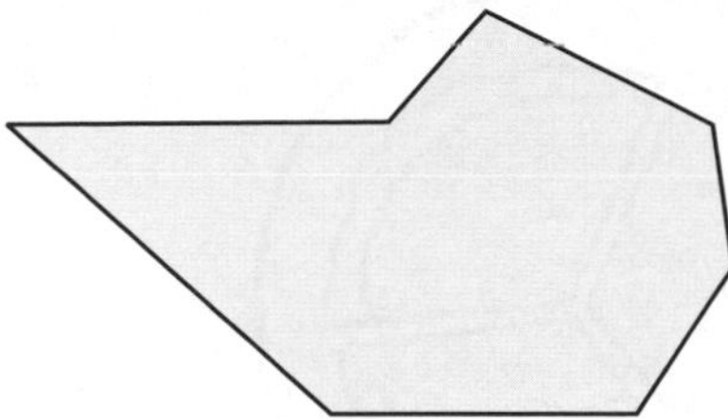

1 mark

4 Draw the following angles using a ruler and a protractor.

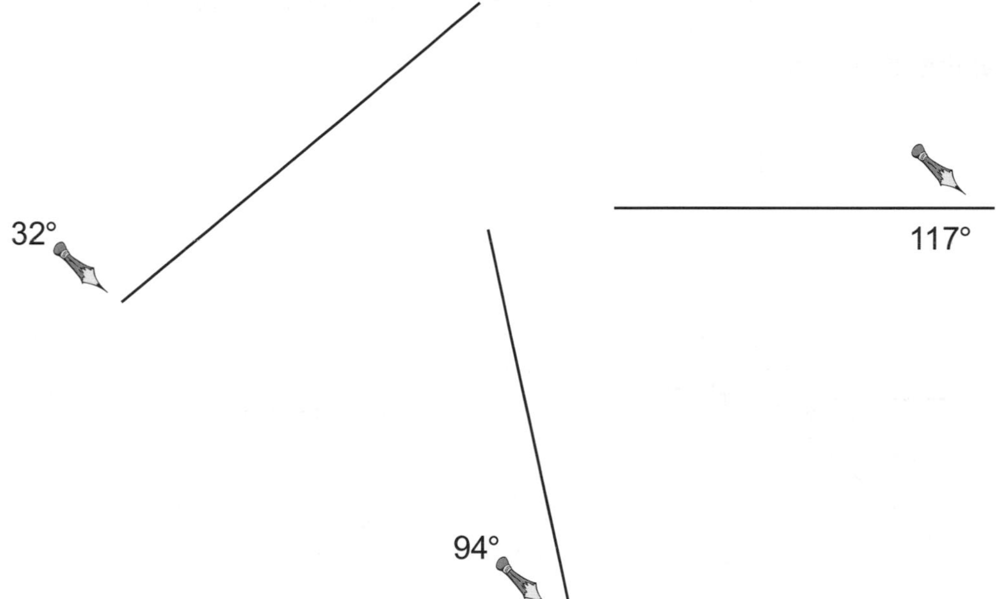

3 marks

5 Without measuring them, say which of these angles is 60°.

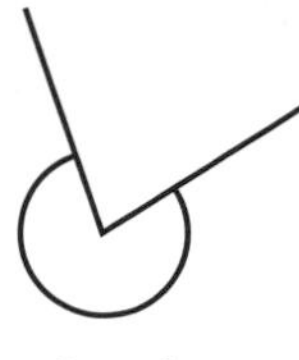

Angle w

Angle x

Angle y

Angle z

Angle

1 mark

"I know that angles are measured in degrees. I can estimate, measure and draw angles. I can identify acute, obtuse, reflex and right angles."

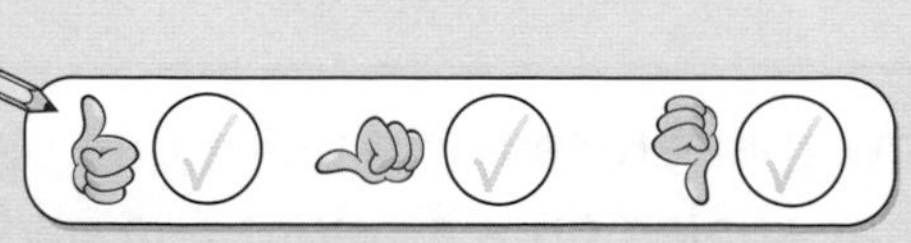

Angle Rules

1 This pie has been cut into 3 equal slices.

Without using a protractor, work out the value of angle x.

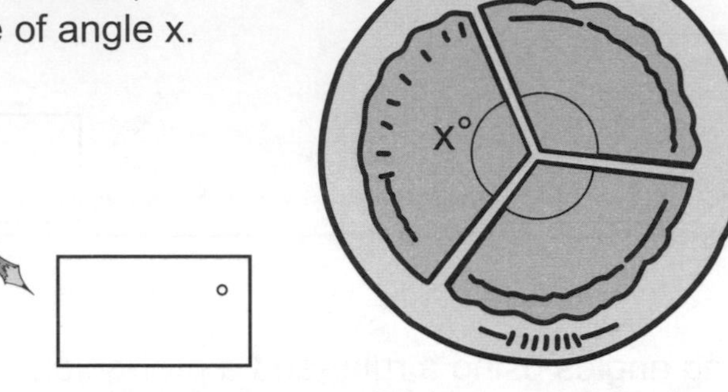

°

1 mark

2 Look at this diagram.

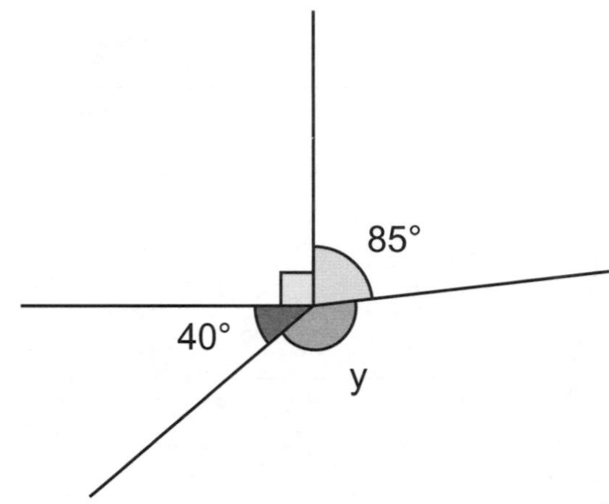

Calculate angle y.

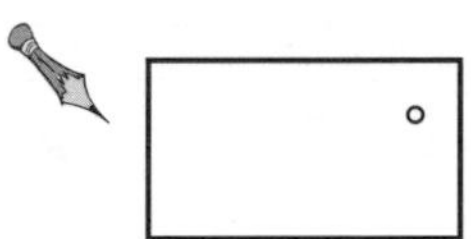

1 mark

3 The angle between the minute hand and the hour hand is 150°.

What angle does the hour hand need to turn to reach 6 o'clock?

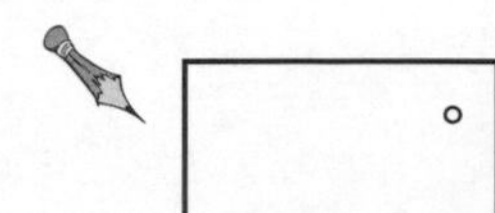

1 mark

"I know that angles at a point add up to 360° and that angles on a straight line add up to 180°."

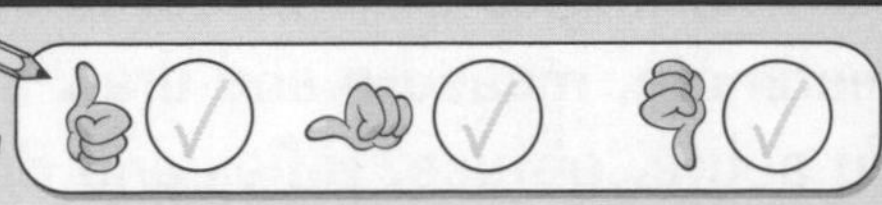

Angle Rules

4 Look at this diagram.

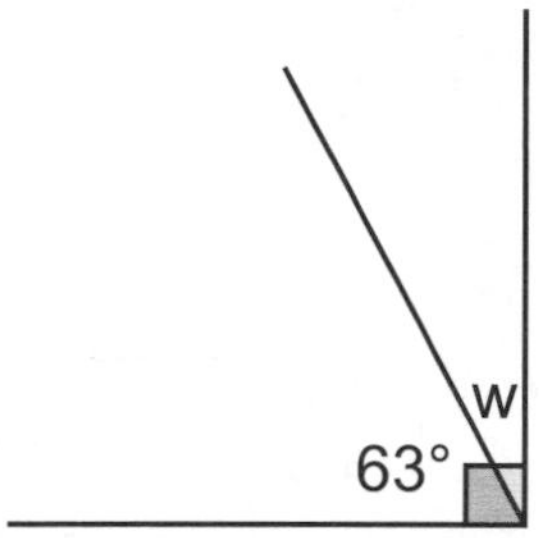

w

63°

Calculate angle w.

°

1 mark

5 Look at this diagram.

Calculate angle f.

°

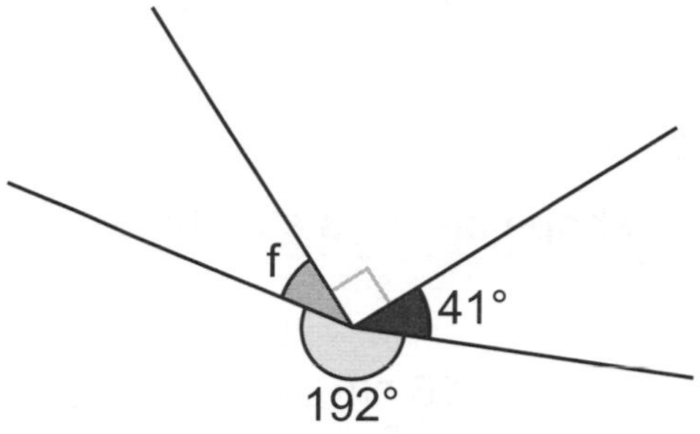

f

41°

192°

1 mark

6 Jo has baked a cake. Tom eats a quarter of it.

Jo takes the rest of the cake.
She cuts one slice measuring 25° and one slice measuring 59°.
Calculate how much cake Jo has left in degrees.

°

1 mark

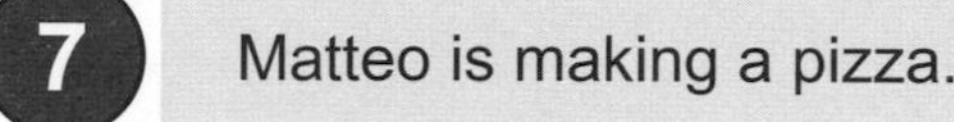

7 Matteo is making a pizza.

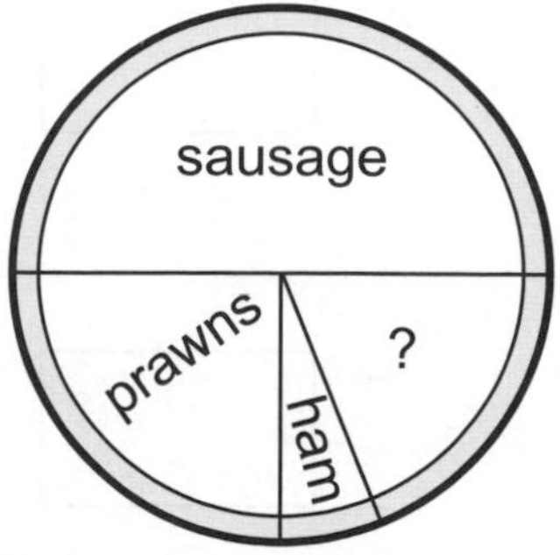

He puts sausage on half of it
and prawns on a quarter of it.
He puts ham on a slice measuring 22°.
How much of the pizza hasn't got any toppings on it?

1 mark

"I know that angles at a ¼ turn add up to 90° and that angles at a ¾ turn add up to 270°."

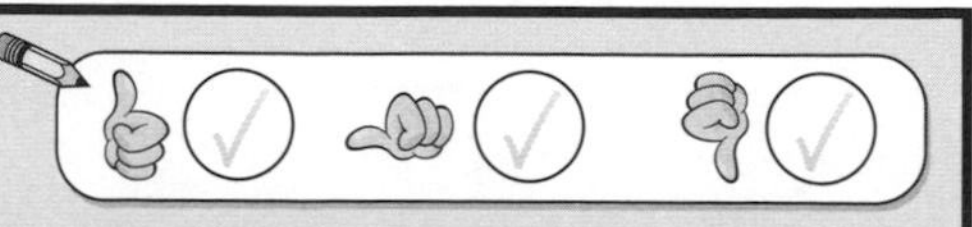

Angles and Sides of Rectangles

1 Look at the rectangle below.

What is the length of side a?

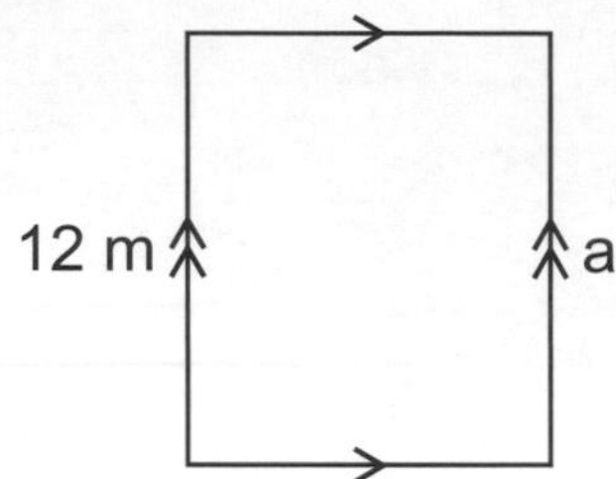

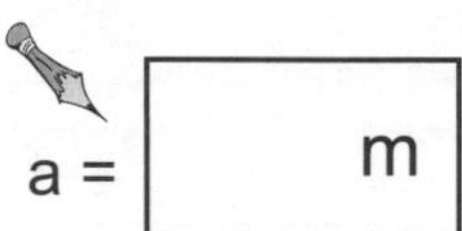

1 mark

2 The shape below is a rectangle.

Side s is half the length of side p.
What is the length of side s?

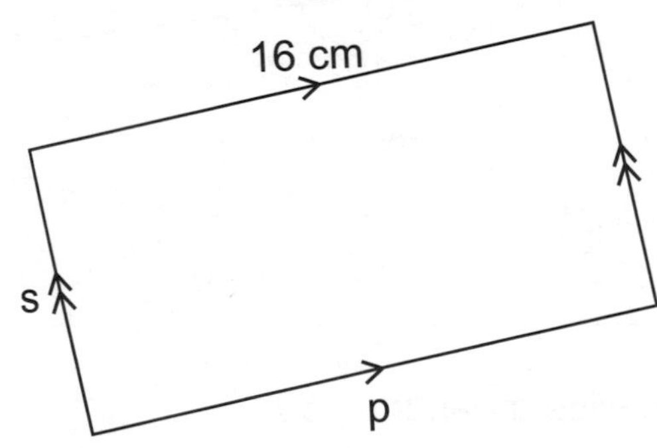

s = cm

1 mark

3 The shape below is a rectangle.

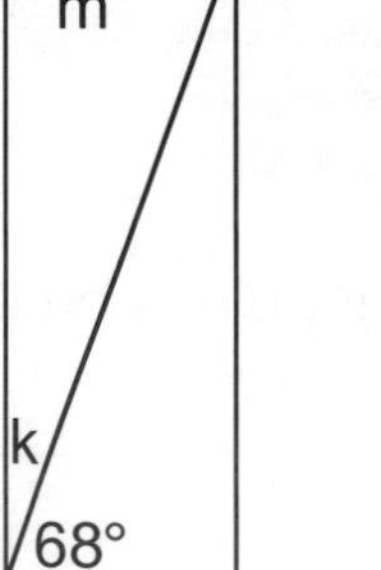

What is the size of angle m?

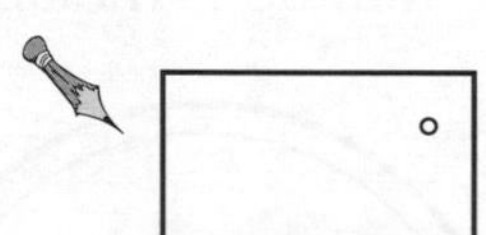

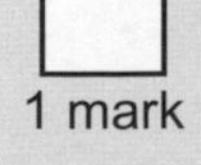
1 mark

Calculate angle k.

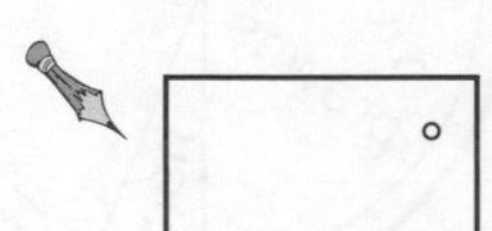

1 mark

Angles and Sides of Rectangles

4 The perimeter of this rectangle is 260 cm.

x

40 cm y

z

What are the lengths of the missing sides? Show your working.

x = cm

y = cm

z = cm

3 marks

5 The perimeter of Rob's garden is 76 m.

27°
q
pond
12 m
path

Rob is building a path along the bottom of his garden.
How long will the path be? Show your working.

m

1 mark

Rob is also building a pond in the corner of his garden.
Calculate angle q.

°

1 mark

"I can use my knowledge of rectangles to work out missing sides and missing angles."

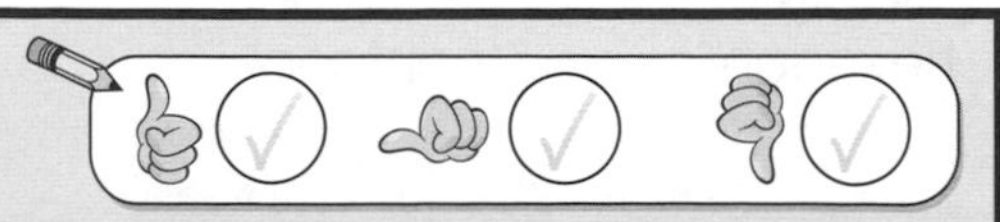

Regular and Irregular Polygons

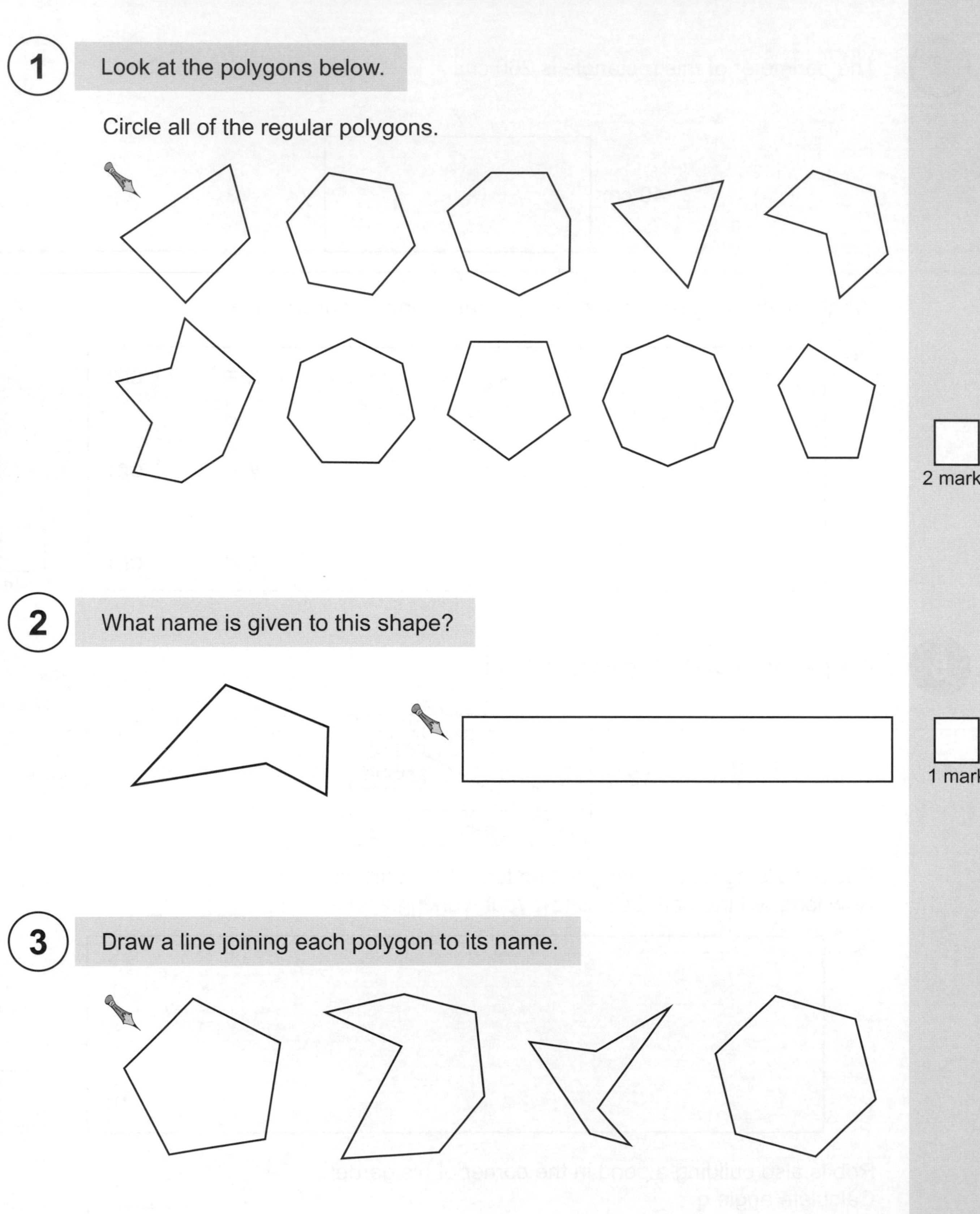

1 Look at the polygons below.

Circle all of the regular polygons.

2 marks

2 What name is given to this shape?

1 mark

3 Draw a line joining each polygon to its name.

regular hexagon | regular pentagon | irregular hexagon | regular octagon | irregular heptagon

2 marks

Regular and Irregular Polygons

4 On the grid provided, draw an irregular heptagon.

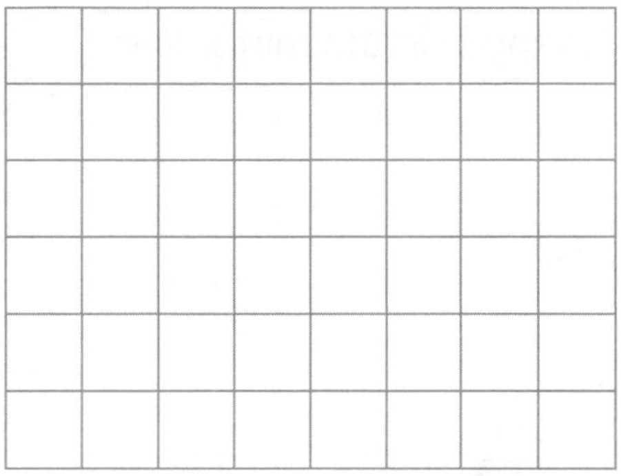

1 mark

5 Look at this octagon.

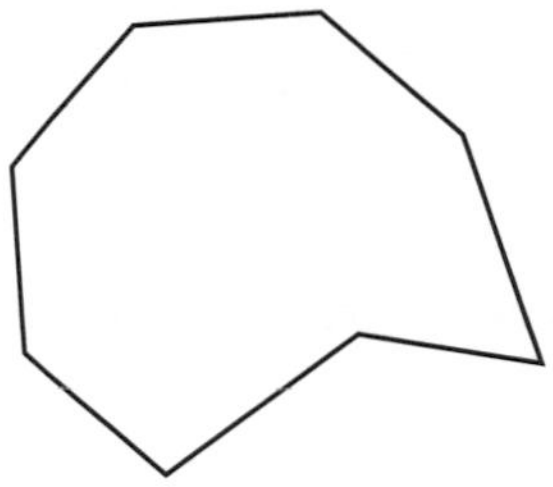

Is it a regular or an irregular octagon?

Give two reasons for your answer.

Reason 1:

Reason 2:

2 marks

6 This shape is a regular nonagon.

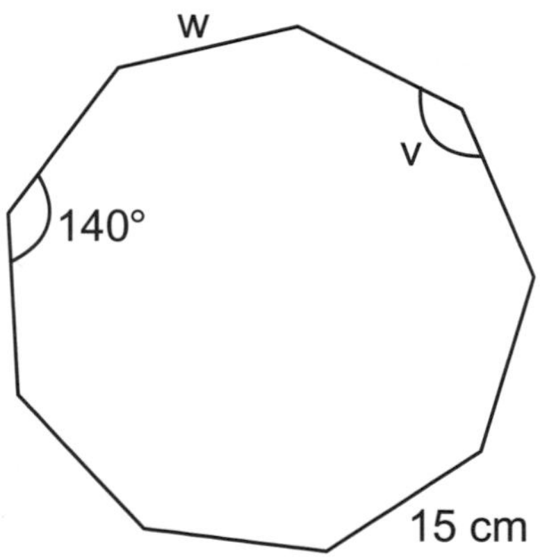

w

v

140°

15 cm

What is the length of side w? cm

1 mark

What is the size of angle v? °

1 mark

"I can tell whether a polygon is regular or irregular based on its sides and its angles."

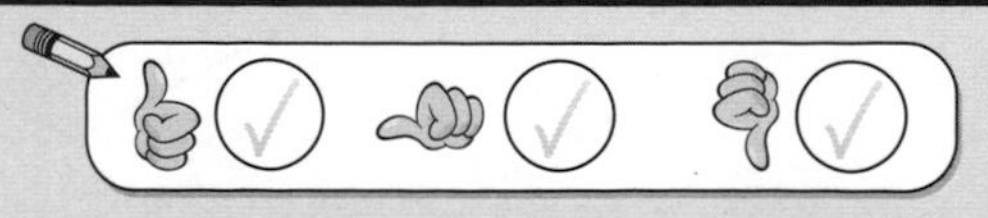

Reflection

1 Shape E is an irregular polygon.

Draw a reflection of Shape E in the mirror line.

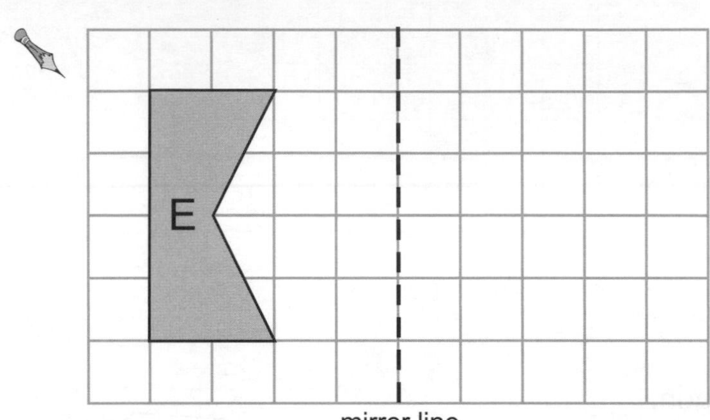

1 mark

2 Shape A is reflected in the mirror line.

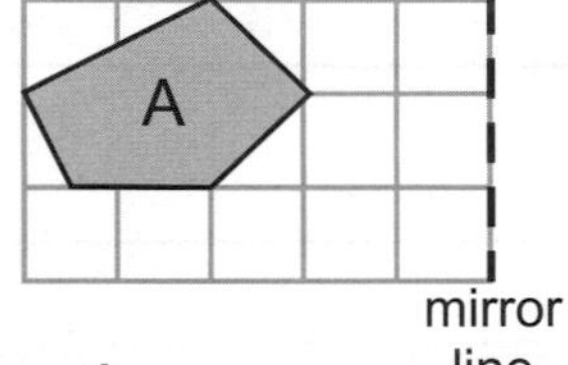

Circle the grid that shows the reflection of Shape A.

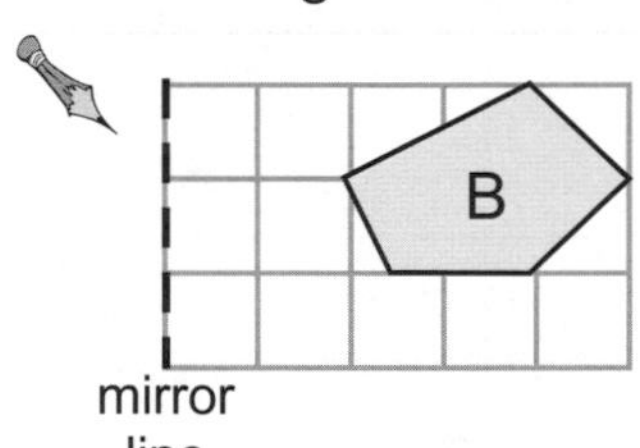

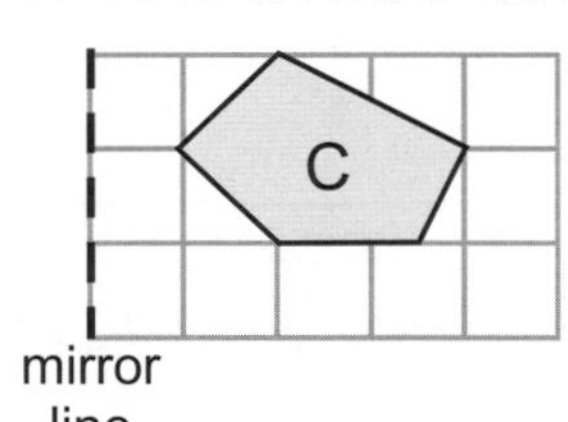

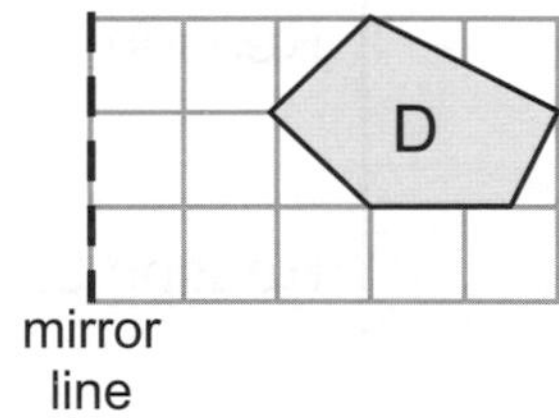

1 mark

3 Shape F is an irregular hexagon.

Draw a reflection of Shape F in the mirror line.

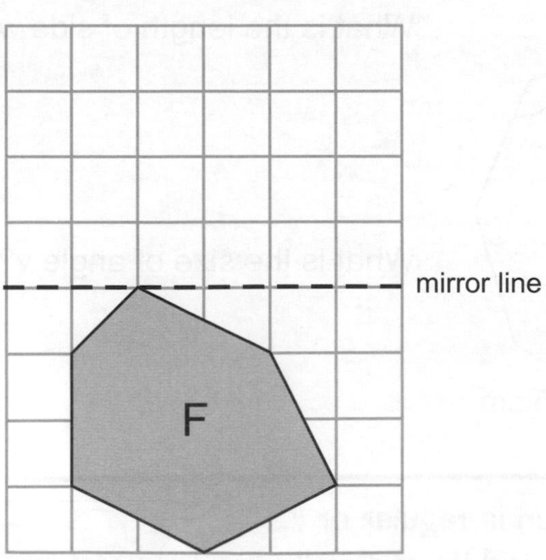

1 mark

Reflection

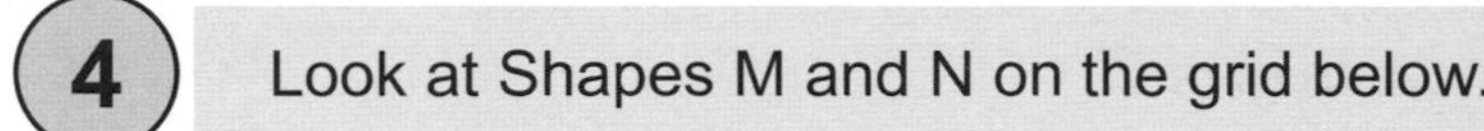

4 Look at Shapes M and N on the grid below.

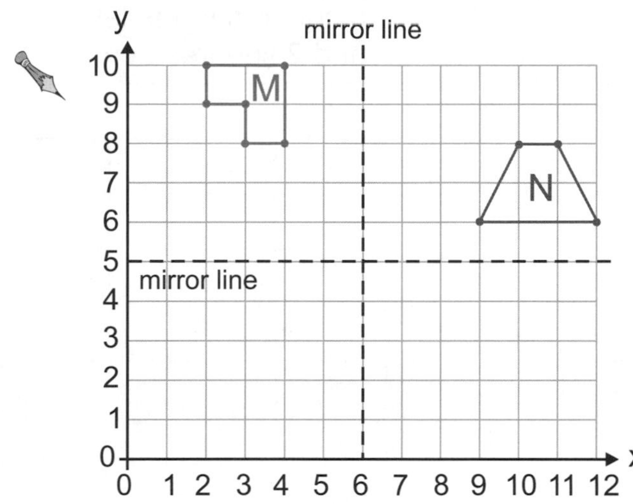

Draw the reflection of Shape M in the vertical mirror line.

1 mark

Draw the reflection of Shape N in the horizontal mirror line.

1 mark

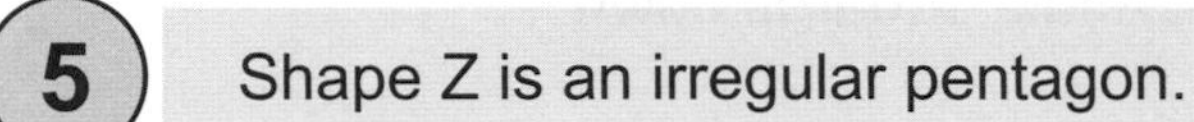

5 Shape Z is an irregular pentagon.

Reflect Shape Z in both mirror lines.

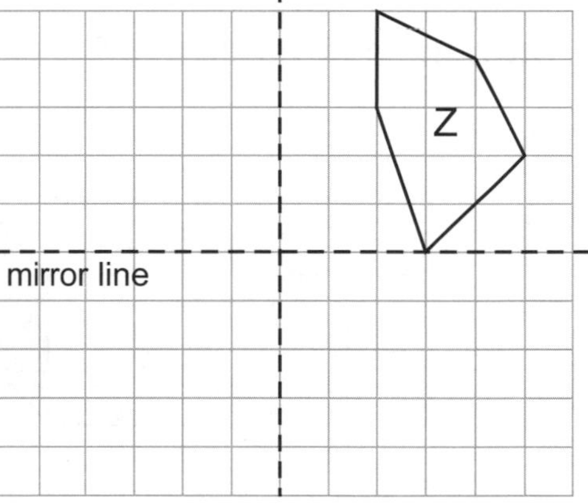

1 mark

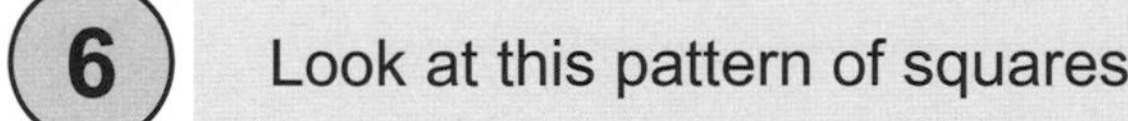

6 Look at this pattern of squares.

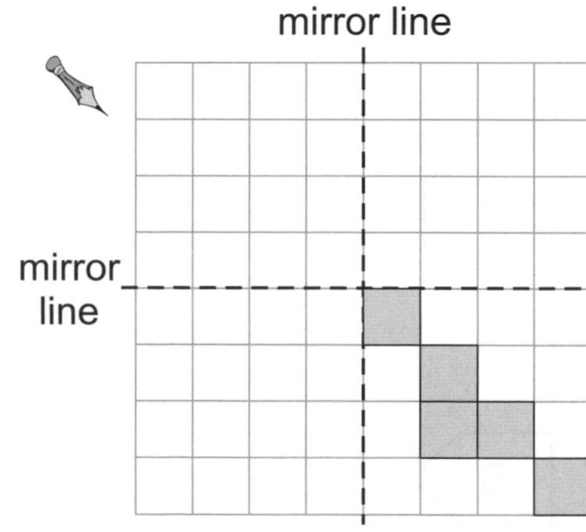

Shade in 15 more squares to make this pattern symmetrical in both mirror lines.

1 mark

"I can draw where a shape will be after it has been reflected in a mirror line."

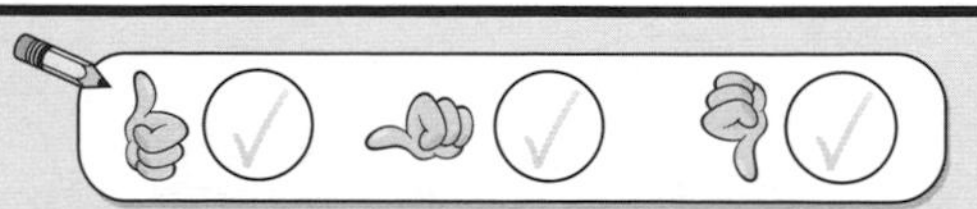

Translation

1 Translate these shapes by the amounts given.

4 squares to the right.

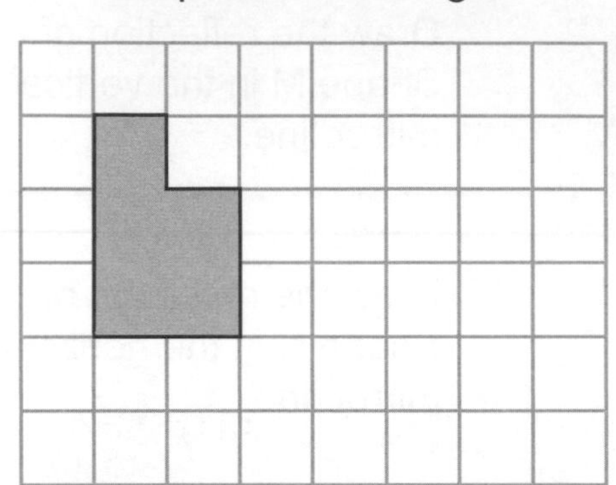

5 squares to the left and 2 squares down.

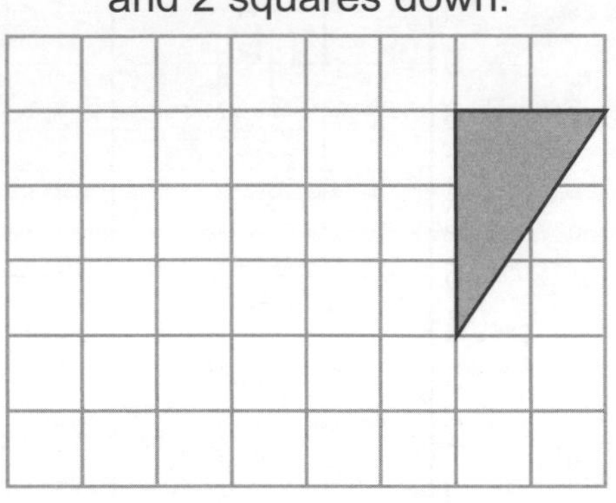

2 marks

2 Shape A is translated 4 squares to the right and 2 squares down.

Draw the new position of Shape A.

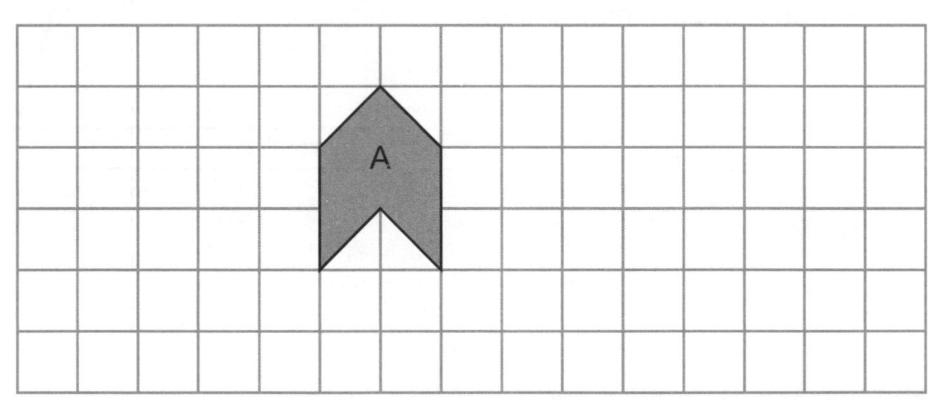

1 mark

3 Translate Shape B 2 squares to the right and 4 squares up.

Draw your answer on the grid.

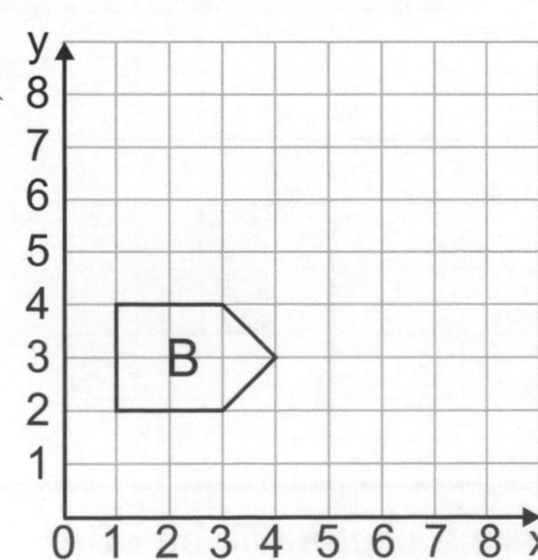

1 mark

Translation

4 Look at the shapes on this grid.

Translate Shape E three squares to the right. Draw its new position and label your Shape F.

1 mark

Translate Shape G two squares to the left and one square down. Draw its new position and label it H.

1 mark

5 Lloyd wants to move his bed to a new place.

He moves his bed from place A to place B. Describe this move as a translation.

[ ] squares [ ]

and [ ] squares [ ]

1 mark

The bed is now at place B.
Lloyd translates it 4 squares left and 2 squares up.
Draw the bed in its new place on the grid. Label it C.

1 mark

6 Hasan and Gena are playing chess.

= Hasan's piece = Gena's piece

Gena moves her piece 1 square to the right and 2 squares up. Draw the piece in its new position.

1 mark

Hasan wants to move his piece so that it's in the same position as Gena's piece. Describe this move as a translation.

1 mark

"I can identify and draw where a shape will be after a translation. I can describe translations."

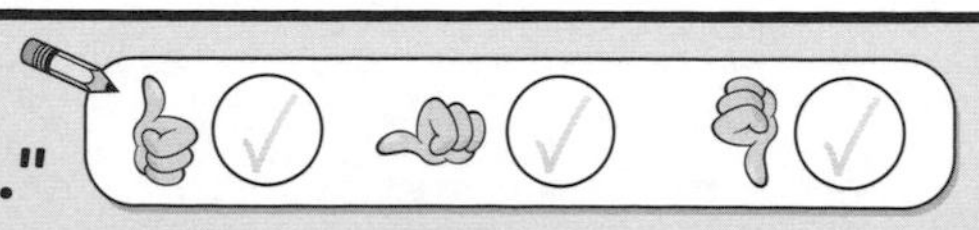

Line Graphs

Jack and Sam measure their height each year.
They plot a line graph of their results.

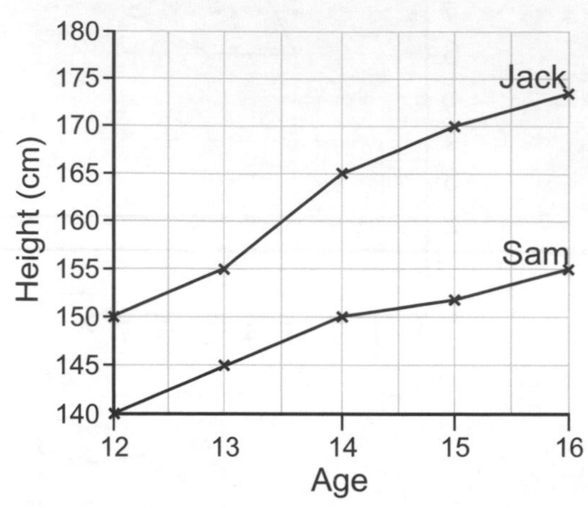

How tall was Jack when he was 14 years old?

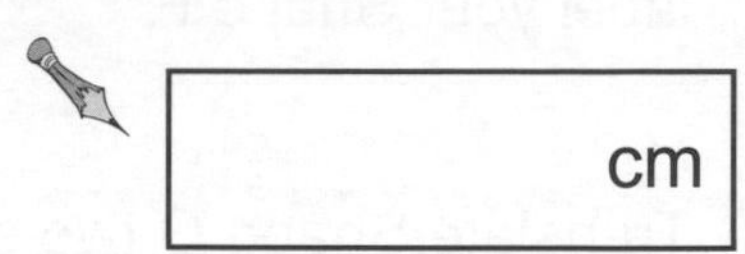

1 mark

How much taller was Jack than Sam when they were both 13 years old?

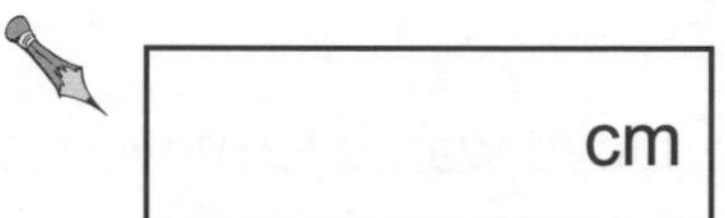

1 mark

2 This graph shows the number of umbrellas sold by a shop over a year.

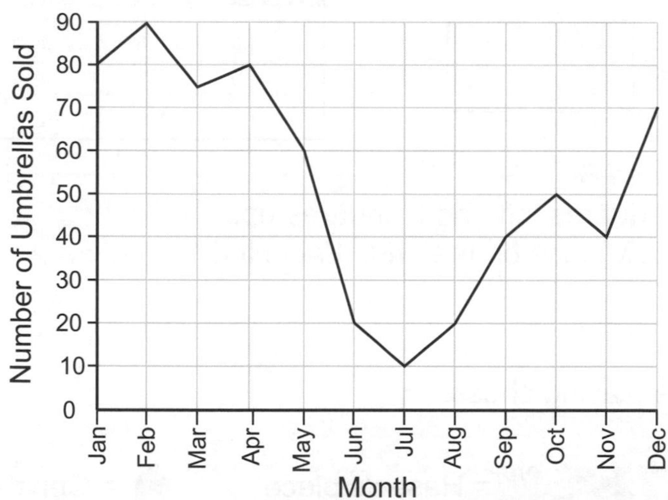

How many umbrellas were sold in March?

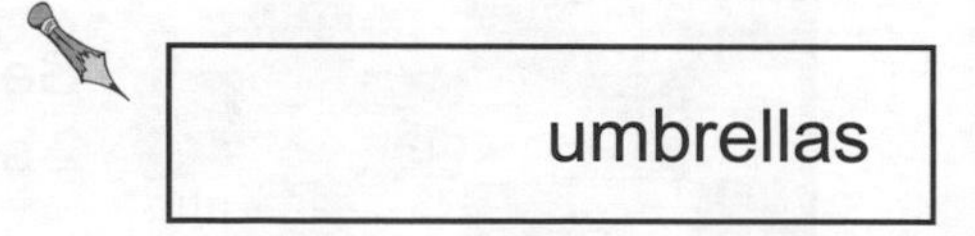

1 mark

How many more umbrellas did the shop sell in November than they sold in July?

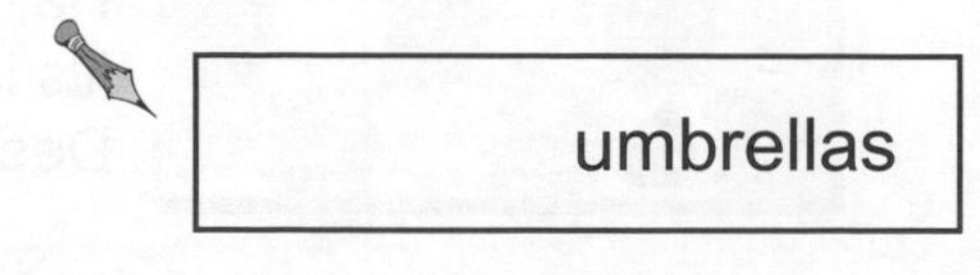

1 mark

How many umbrellas were sold in total in August, September and October?

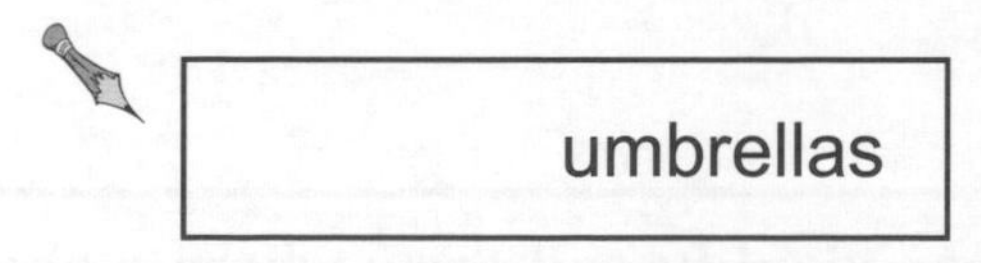

1 mark

Line Graphs

Toby heated a pan of soup on a large ring on the cooker.
His sister Liz heated a pan of soup on a small ring.

The line graph shows the rise in temperature of each pan of soup.

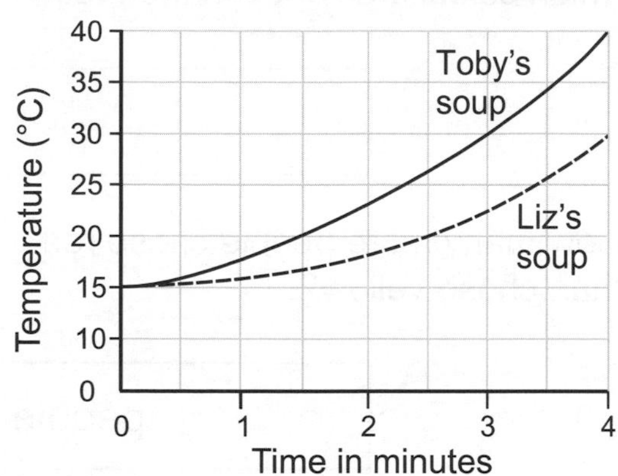

What was the temperature of Liz's soup after 2.5 minutes?

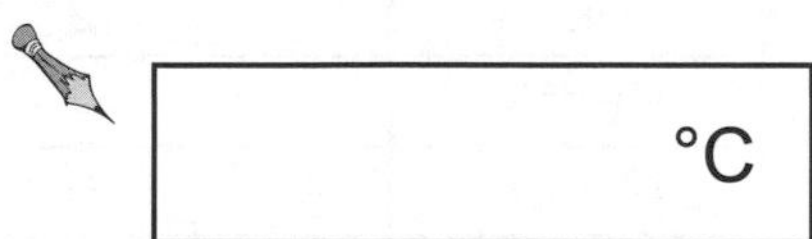

1 mark

How long did it take for Toby's soup to warm up to 30 °C?

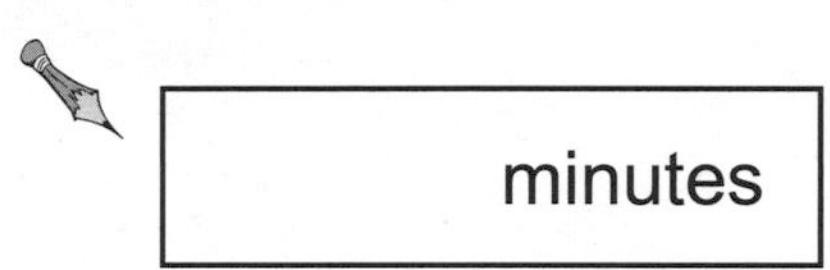

1 mark

How many degrees warmer was Toby's soup than Liz's soup after 4 minutes?

1 mark

4

Christie ran 100 metres. This graph shows how far he ran over time.

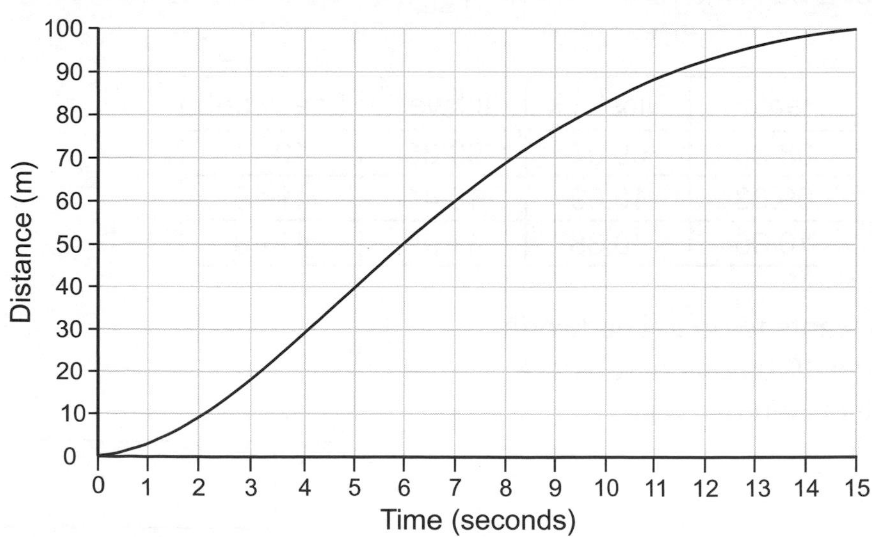

How much longer did it take him to run the last 50 m compared to the first 50 m?

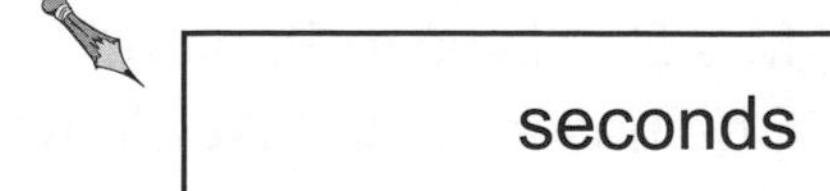

1 mark

"I can solve problems using data from a line graph."

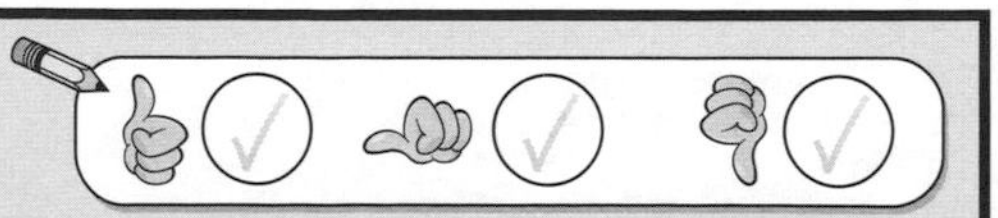

Tables and Timetables

1 Vicky asked her friends to choose their favourite colour from a list.

She made a table of how many people chose each colour.

Colour	Number of People
Red	6
Yellow	2
Purple	4
Green	9
Blue	3

Which colour was chosen the most?

1 mark

How many more people chose red than chose yellow?

people

1 mark

2 Tom asks 40 children how they travel to school.

Fill in the missing number in the table below.

Method of Travel	Car	Bus	Walking
Number of Children	13		20

1 mark

3 Here is part of a bus timetable.

Penton	Nibstock	Inkwell	Leadworth
08.38	09.07	09.35	10.11
09.33	10.09	10.41	11.19
10.06	10.38	11.09	11.48

Mr Writewell wants to go to Leadworth.
He catches the 10.09 bus at Nibstock.
How long will his journey take?

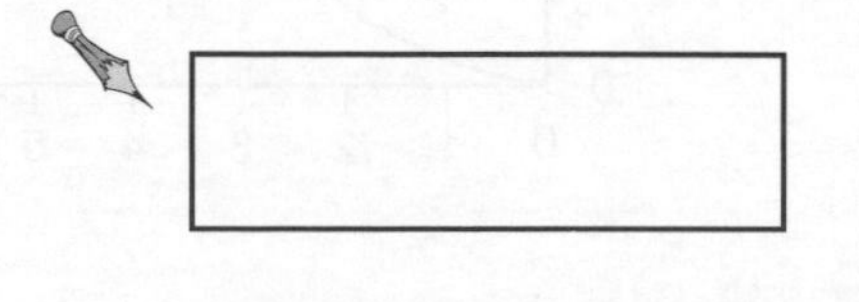

1 mark

Mrs Blot lives in Penton.
She has to be in Inkwell by 10.30.
Which bus should she catch?

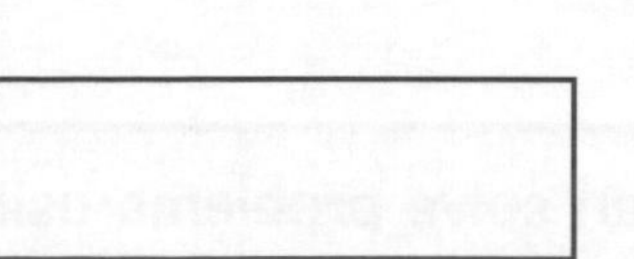

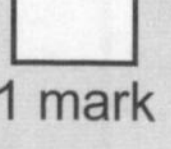

1 mark

Tables and Timetables

4 Evan is travelling by train to Carlisle.

Haltwhistle	16.22	17.14	17.56	18.24
Brampton	16.37	17.29	18.11	18.39
Wetheral	16.46	17.38	18.20	18.48
Carlisle	17.02	17.54	18.36	19.04

How long does it take to travel between Haltwhistle and Wetheral?

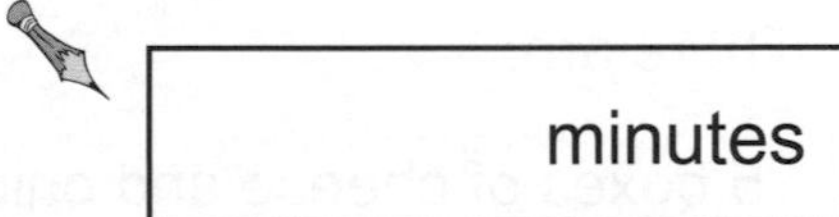

1 mark

Evan catches the 17.29 train at Brampton but the train is 17 minutes late.
At what time does Evan arrive in Carlisle?

1 mark

A train leaves Brampton at 22.05. When does it arrive at Wetheral?

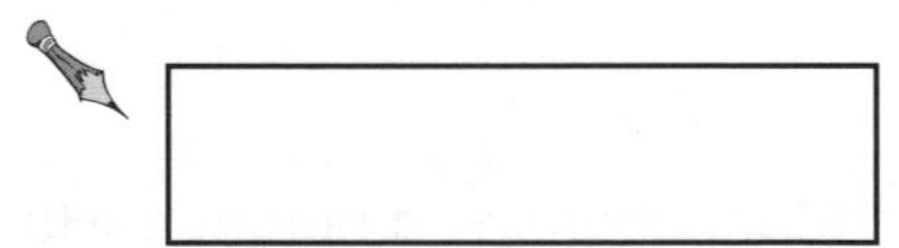

1 mark

5 Five children took a maths test which was out of 100 marks.

Janet scored 5 fewer marks than Ahmed.
Freddie scored twice as many marks as Mike.
Sara scored 28 more marks than the lowest mark of the group.

Use this information to complete the table of their results.

Name	Ahmed	Freddie	Janet	Mike	Sara
Mark	64			34	

2 marks

"I can complete, read and interpret information in tables and timetables."

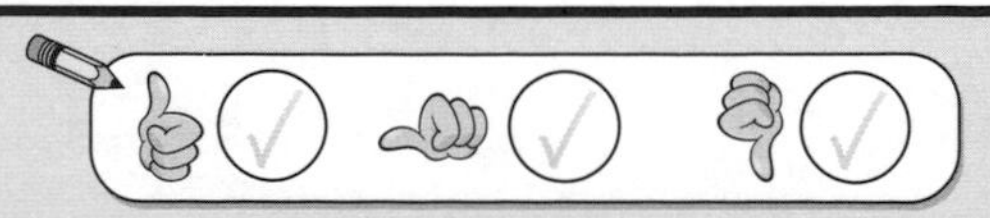

Year Five Objectives Test

1 Fill in the empty box.

7600 ÷ [ ] = 76

1 mark

2 In a school shop there are some boxes of crisps.
Each box contains 30 packets of crisps.

There are:

5 boxes of cheese and onion flavour

4 boxes of beef flavour

6 boxes of chicken flavour

How many packets of crisps are there altogether? Show your working.

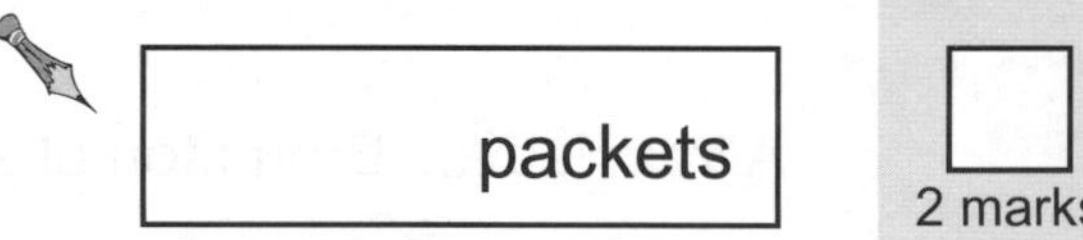

2 marks

3 Mark chooses a number. He multiplies it by 3 then subtracts 12.
The answer is 21.

What number did Mark choose?

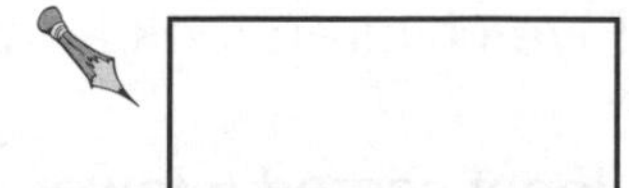

1 mark

4 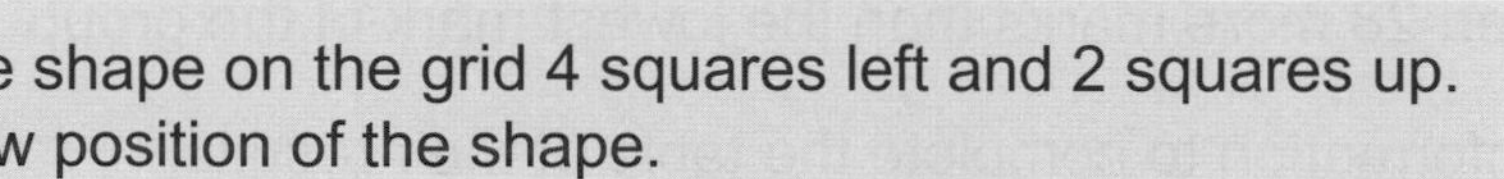
Translate the shape on the grid 4 squares left and 2 squares up.
Draw the new position of the shape.

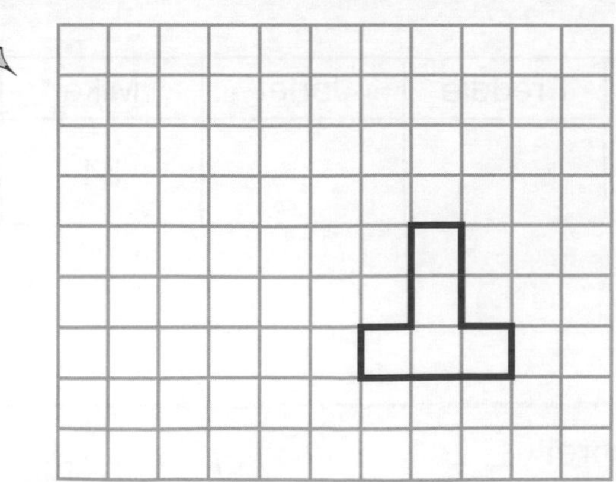

1 mark

Here are four digit cards.

Use two of the digit cards to make a multiple of 4.

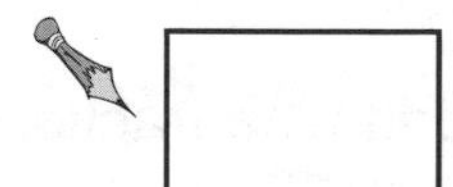

1 mark

Use two of the digit cards to make a square number.

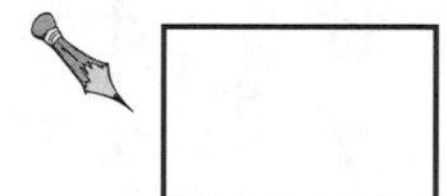

1 mark

6

The graph shows the number of bikes sold in a shop each month.

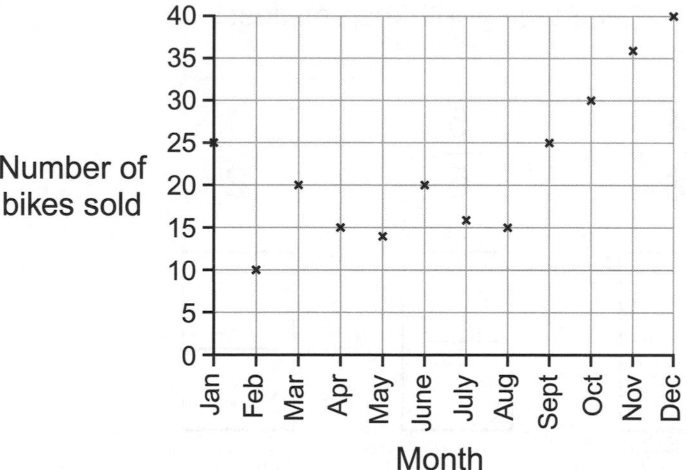

How many months on the graph show sales of less than 15 bikes?

1 mark

What is the difference between the number of bikes sold in June and the number of bikes sold in October?

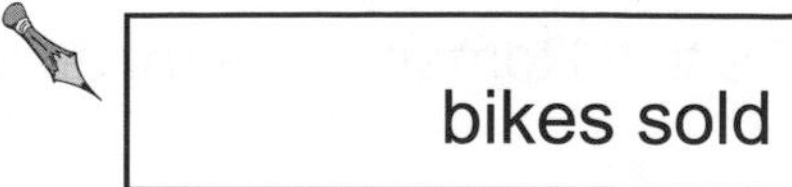

1 mark

7 45 043 fans go to a football match to watch Barrow FC.

Round this number to the nearest 10 000.

1 mark

8 Add these fractions, giving your answer as a mixed number.

$$\frac{6}{7} + \frac{4}{7}$$

2 marks

9 Write these fractions in size order, starting with the smallest.

$\frac{3}{4}$ $\frac{4}{6}$ $\frac{5}{6}$ $\frac{1}{2}$

smallest ⟶ largest

1 mark

10 Write this Roman numeral as a number.

MCCLXVIII

1 mark

11 Alfred buys two new cars, costing £8465 and £4632.

How much do they cost in total?

£

1 mark

12 Circle the fraction that is equivalent to 0.55.

$\frac{5}{11}$ $\frac{55}{1000}$ $\frac{3}{8}$ $\frac{55}{10}$ $\frac{55}{100}$

1 mark

13 Complete this multiplication using three prime numbers.

☐ × ☐ × ☐ = 42

1 mark

14 Rob drives the same journey five times a month.
At the end of each month he has driven 1065 miles.

How far is each journey?

miles

1 mark

Each journey uses 44 pints of petrol.
How much petrol does Rob use a month?
Give your answer in litres. 1 litre is approximately 2 pints.

litres

2 marks

Total

Answers

Pages 2-5 — Year Four Objectives Test

Q1 **2** *(1 mark)*

Q2 E.g:

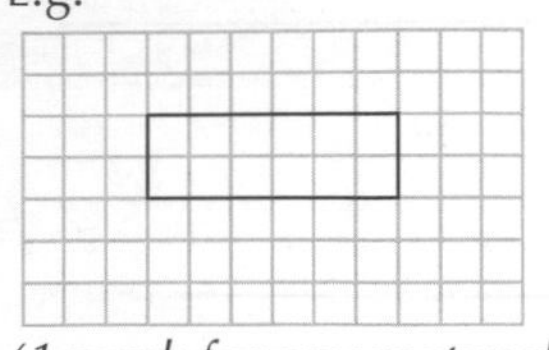

(1 mark for any rectangle covering 12 squares.)

Q3 **19:25** *(1 mark)*
1 hour = 60 minutes
Quarter of an hour = 15 minutes
60 + 15 = **75 minutes**
(1 mark)

Q4 She spent: 48 + 25 = 73p
She had: 50 + 20 + 20 = 90p
90 – 73 = 17p
She has **17p** left
(2 marks for correct answer, otherwise 1 mark for attempting to subtract 73p.)

Q5 **0.1** *(1 mark)*

Q6 I = 1
X = 10
C = 100
100 – 10 + 2 = **92**
(1 mark)
X = 10
I = 1
10 – 1 + 10 = **19**
(1 mark)

Q7 0.45 × 1000 = **450 m**
(1 mark)

Q8 The temperature difference between 25 °C and 0 °C is 25 °C.
The temperature difference between 0 °C and –12 °C is 12 °C.
So the difference between 25 °C and –12 °C is 25 + 12 = **37 °C** *(1 mark)*

Q9 18 – 12 = **6** more salami pizzas were sold on Saturday. *(1 mark)*
9 × 2 = **18** ham pizzas were sold on Friday.
(1 mark)

Q10 **0.07**, **0.11**, **0.16**, **1.44**, **5.15**, **23.04** *(1 mark)*

Q11 $\mathbf{\frac{6}{8}}$, $\mathbf{\frac{1}{3}}$ and $\mathbf{\frac{9}{18}}$
(2 marks for all correct, otherwise 1 mark for 2 correct.)

Q12 Top number: **6**
Bottom number: **8**
(1 mark for both correct.)

Q13
$$\begin{array}{r} 25.4 \\ +\ 6.7 \\ \hline 32.1 \\ \hline {}_{1\,1} \end{array}$$

So he kicked the ball **32.1 m**. *(1 mark)*

Q14 72 ÷ 6 = 12
12 × 5 = **60** *(1 mark)*

Q15 4 + 2 + 2 + 2 + 2 + 4 + 2 + 4 + 2 = **24 cm** *(1 mark)*

Section One — Number and Place Value

Page 6 — Counting Backwards Through Zero

Q1 **2** *(1 mark)*
–3 *(1 mark)*

Q2 **8 °C** *(1 mark)*
–6 °C *(1 mark)*

Q3 **–14 °C** *(1 mark)*

Q4 **38 °C** *(1 mark)*

Page 7 — Place Value in Big Numbers

Q1 **4 thousands** *(1 mark)*
6 hundred thousands
(1 mark)
2 tens *(1 mark)*

Q2 **One hundred and twenty six thousand, five hundred and forty seven pounds** *(1 mark)*

Q3 **5 248 063** *(1 mark)*
711 907 *(1 mark)*

Q4 89490 = **80 000** + **9000** + 400 + **90** *(1 mark)*

Page 8 — Ordering and Comparing Big Numbers

Q1 217 563 < 271 236
575 896 < 758 962
924 567 > 924 537
223 237 < 224 237
(2 marks for all correct, otherwise 1 mark for 3 correct.)

Q2 **Year 1** *(1 mark)*
Year 3 *(1 mark)*
< *(1 mark)*

Q3 **21 989**, **216 452**, **217 569**, **318 569**
(1 mark)